124404

D1105020

Wonderful Wizard

Marvelous Land

813
M782
c.2

onderful

izard

arvelous

and

by
Raylyn Moore

Preface
by
Ray Bradbury

Bowling Green University Popular Press
Bowling Green, Ohio 43403

Copyright © 1974 by Raylyn Moore
          Bowling Green University Popular Press,
          Ray B. Browne, Editor. The Bowling Green University
          Popular Press is the publishing division of the Center for
          the Study of Popular Culture, Ray B. Browne, Director.

ISBN: 0-87972-068-9 CB
       0-87972-069-7 PB

Library of Congress No. 74-78787

LEWIS & CLARK LIBRARY SYSTEM
         P. O. BOX 368
    EDWARDSVILLE, ILL. 62025

To my daughter, Sara Rivkeh Moore, who from the age of six has contributed valuable insights about Oz.

131943

Acknowledgements

Thanks to those who helped, including my husband Ward Moore, who allowed me to draw without reservation on his enthusiasm for the subject and his remembrance of times past; my literary agent Virginia Kidd, who acted on behalf of this project in a particularly selfless way that transcends the ordinary function of agentry; the staff at Pacific Grove (California) Public Library, who performed impossible feats of acquiring pertinent material; Dr. Abraham Bezanker of the Department of English, San Jose State University, who served as adviser; Felix Severance, Charles Polk, Pat Carey et al., who offered and lent hard-to-get early Baum books; Stella Zamvil who performed emergency errands out of friendship, and Brenda and Norman Wallace, who kept my car running by thaumaturgy.

CONTENTS

ecause because .....

by Ray Bradbury

he Banm boom

anm's life and art

he imaginary continent

BECAUSE, BECAUSE, BECAUSE

BECAUSE OF THE WONDERFUL THINGS HE DOES

A Preface

≫≫ LET US CONSIDER TWO AUTHORS WHOSE BOOKS WERE burned in our American society during the past 70 years. Librarians and teachers did the burning very subtly by not buying. And not buying is as good as burning. Yet, the authors survived.

Two gentlemen of no talent whatsoever.

Two mysteries of literature, if you can call their work literature.

Two men who changed the world somewhat more than they ever dreamed, once they were in it, once their books came to be published and moved in the minds and blood of 8 year olds, 10 year olds, 12 year olds.

One of them changed the future of the entire world and that Universe which waited for Earthmen to birth themselves in space with rockets.

His name: Edgar Rice Burroughs. His John Carter grew to maturity two generations of astronomers, geologists, bio-chemists, and astronauts who cut their teeth on his Barsoomian beasts and Martian fighting men and decided to grow up and grow out away from Earth.

The second man, also a "mediocre" talent, if you can believe the teachers and librarians of some 70 years, created a country, Oz, and peopled it with not one influence, but several dozens.

His name: L. Frank Baum.

And once you begin to name his people in his country, it is hard to stop: Dorothy, Toto (indeed a very real person), The Tin Man, The Scarecrow, Tik-Tok, Ozma, Polychrome, The Patchwork Girl, Ruggedo, Prof. Wogglebug, Aunty Em, The Wicked Witch of the ————. You see how easily the names pop out, without having to go look them up!

Two mysteries, then. One the mystery of growing boys to men by romanticizing their taffy bones so the damn things *rise* toward the sun, no, toward Mars. Now, let us set Mr. Burroughs aside.

Let us get on with the mystery of L. Frank Baum, that faintly old-maidish man who grew boys inward to their most delightful interiors, kept them home, and romanced them with wonders between their ears.

And this book is, of course, about the latter mystery, the mystery of that strange dear little Wizard Himself. The man who wanted to work magic but, oh dear, not *hurt* anyone along the way. He is that rare chef who would never dream to yell at his cooks, yet got results anyway: a bakery-kitchen full of valentines, sweet-meats, dragons without teeth, robots with feelings, Tin Men who were once real (to reverse the Pinocchio myth), and girls who are so toothsome and innocent that if you nibble them at all, it would only be their toes, ears, and elbows.

It is a book about a man compelled to money, but saved by his secret self, his hidden creative person.

It is a book about a man who set out, unknowingly, to slaughter his own best talents, but was saved by a mob of strange creatures from another land who knew better than he that they needed to be born. And in birthing themselves insured the miraculous fact that if we all went to the nearest travel agency tomorrow and were asked if we wanted to go to Alice's Wonderland or The Emerald City, it would be that Green Place, and the Munchkins and the Quadlings and all the rest, every time!

It is fascinating to compare memories of Dorothy and Oz and Baum with Alice and the Looking Glass and the Rabbit Hole and Lewis Carroll, who made out better with librarians and teachers.

When we think of Oz a whole mob of incredibly lovely if strange people falls across our minds.

When we think of Alice's encounters we think of mean, waspish, small, carping, bad-mannered children ranting against *going* to bed, refusing to get *out* of bed, not liking the food, hating the temperature, minding the weather out of mind.

If Love is the lubricant that runs Oz to glory, Hate is the mud in which all sink to ruin inside the mirror where poor Alice is trapped.

If everyone goes around democratically accepting each other's foibles in the four lands surrounding the Emerald City, and feeling nothing but amiable wonder toward such eccentricities as pop up, the reverse is true when Alice meets a Caterpillar or Tweedledum and Tweedledee or assorted knights, Queens, and Old Women. Theirs is an aristocracy of snobs, no one is good enough for them. They themselves are crazy eccentrics, but eccentricity in anyone else is beyond comprehension and should best be guillotined or grown small and stepped on.

Both books, both authors, stay in our minds, for mirror-reversed reasons. We float and fly through Oz on grand winds that make us beautiful kites. We trudge and fight our way through Wonderland, amazed that we survive at all.

Wonderland, for all its fantasy, is most practically real, that world where people have conniption fits and knock you out of line on your way onto a bus.

Oz is that place, ten minutes before sleep, where we bind up our wounds, soak our feet, dream ourselves better, snooze poetry on our lips, and decide that mankind, for all it's snide and mean and dumb, must be given another chance come dawn and a hearty breakfast.

Oz is muffins and honey, summer vacations, and all the easy green time in the world.

Wonderland is cold gruel and arithmetic at six a.m., icy showers, long schools.

It is not surprising that Wonderland is the darling of the intellectuals.

It is similarly not surprising that dreamers and intuitionists would reject the cold mirror of Carroll and take their chances on hotfooting it over the forbidden desert which at least promises utter destruction for purely inanimate reasons (the desert, after all, is not alive and doesn't know whom it is destroying), heading for Oz. Because in Oz of course reside amiable villains who are really not villains at all. Ruggedo is a fraud and a sham, for all his shouts and leaping about and uttering curses. Whereas Wonderland's Queen of Hearts really *does* chop off heads and children are beaten if they sneeze.

Wonderland is what we Are.

Oz is what we would hope and like to be.

The distance between raw animal and improved human can be measured by pegging a line between Alice's Rabbit Hole and Dorothy's Yellow Brick Road.

One need not polarize oneself by picking one country, one heroine, one set of characters. It is not either-or, or this or that. It can be both.

It is the sad/happy state of mankind always to be making such measurements: where we are as against where we would like to be.

I hope that the lovers of Wonderland and the lovers of Oz do not break up into permanent warring camps. That would be foolish and fruitless, for growing humanity needs proper doses of reality and proper doses of dreaming. I would like to believe Alice puts antibodies in our blood to help us survive Reality by showing us as the fickle, reckless, abrupt and alarming children we are. Children, of course, recognize themselves in the mostly bad-mannered grotesques that amble, stalk, and wander up to Alice.

But mean and loud and dreadful make for high tea lacking vitamins. Reality is an unsubstantial meal. Children also recognize a good dream when they see it, and so turn to Mr. Baum for the richer cake rather than the swamp gruel, for the mean-spirit that is really Santa Claus pretending at horrible. Children are willing to risk being smothered in true marmalade and saccharine. Mr. Baum provides both, with some narrow escapes from the maudlin and the thing we damn as sentimentality.

No matter if Mr. Baum was his own worst enemy, or so it seems from reading Raylyn Moore's text. The more he tried to be commercial, the more his intuitive self seemed to pop to the surface saying, finally, "To hell with you, I'm going *my* way!" And away it went, dragging Mr. Baum screaming after it, he yelling for money, his Muse settling for warm creations. Ironically, if Mr. B. had relaxed more, and let the Muse drag him, he would probably have wound up wiser, happier, richer.

I suddenly realize I have been writing part of her book for Raylyn Moore, which was surely not my intention, but that funny thing happened on my way into this Introduction: Mr. Carroll fell by and collided with Mr. Baum. In the resultant scramble, I was locked in and only now fight free.

What you have here, in the following pages, is an attempt made by one of the first people, late in time, to pay attention to a spirited man with a nice old grandma's soul. It is an endeavor to "unburn" the histories of Oz, and shelve the Works where they have rarely, in the history of our country, been shelved: in libraries.

It is not the task of a writer of Prefaces to criticise or super-analyze the work at hand. If Raylyn Moore has done nothing else but begin to stir up some sort of small tempest concerning Oz and the super evident fact it has stood, unassailed and beautific somewhere beyond Kansas for seventy-odd years, her task will have been commendable.

For Oz has not fallen, has it? Even though legions of bright people with grand good taste, and thousands of librarians have fired cannonades in tandem with hosts of sociologists who fear that the mighty Wizard will pollute their children, Baum, across the years, simply reaches in his pocket and produces, Shaggy Man that he is, the Love Magnet.

And if he is not the Shaggy Man, which he surely is, he is the Pied Piper who takes the adoring children away from their dull and unappreciative parents. Let the older folk survive into starvation with their algebra breakfasts, mathematical luncheons, and computer-data-fact dinners. To the children, Baum cries, "Let them eat cake!" but *means* it, and delivers.

In a story of mine published some 22 years ago, *The Exiles*, fine fantasists like Poe and Hawthorne, along with Dickens, and Baum, find themselves shunted off to Mars as the non-dreamers, the super-psychological technicians, the book burners of the future, advance through towns and libraries, tossing the last of the great dreams into the furnace.

At the finale of my story, a rocket arrives on Mars, bearing with it the last copies in existence of Poe and Dickens and Baum. The captain of the ship burns these books on a dead Martian sea-bottom, and Oz at long last crashes over into ruins, Tik-Tok runs to rust, the Wizard and all his dusk-time dreams are destroyed, even as Scrooge, Marley, the Three Spirits, the Raven and the Masque of the Red Death fly away into dusks, gone forever.

I do not for a moment believe that day will ever come. The fight between the dreamers and the fact-finders will continue, and we will embody both in equal proportion, or risk all men singing *castratto* soprano for the literary popes.

I have not predicted futures but, as I have often hopefully pointed out, prevented them. How much has my ounce counted for in a world of data dross?

Who can say? I only know that *1984* is not coming after all. For awhile there we actually thought it might. Man as mere computer-adjunct data collector realist is losing to man as loving companion to a miraculous universe. By such hopes I must live.

Raylyn Moore, if I read her rightly, has given us a book here of such a size and weight as to knock librarians' heads with, and bang sociologists' elbows with, and knock psychiatrists' hats askew. Whether she intends it or not, in sum here I believe her to say, in all truth:

Shakespeare invented Freud.

Hell, Shakespeare invented *everything*!

And long before the first couch was lain upon and the first psychiatrical confession heard.

Baum is a small and inconsequential flower blooming in the shade of Shakespeare. I suppose I will be reviled for mentioning them in one paragraph. But both lived inside their heads with a mind gone wild with wanting, wishing, hoping, shaping, dreaming. There, if no other place, they touch fingertips.

In a world where books are machine-made for "age groups" and pass through dry-parchment analysts' hands before being pill-fed to kids, Baum deserves this book, because Baum is needed. When the cities die, in their present form at least, and we head out into Eden again, which we must and will, Baum will be waiting for us. And if the road we take is not Yellow Brick why, damn it, we can imagine that it is, even as we imagine our wives beautiful and our husbands wise and our children kind until such day as they echo that dream.

When the further critical histories of Oz are written, Raylyn Moore will be proud to know herself as one who raised her voice when, by the thousandfold, others knew their love, but kept it still.

The boy-who-read-the-books inside the man-who-writes-this-preface, thanks her.

Los Angeles, California   Ray Bradbury
July 14, 1973

PART I

The Baum Boom: A New Cult for Old Values

"Never question the truth of what you fail to understand, for the world is filled with wonders."

Speech of the white pearl, *Rinkitink in Oz* (p. 26).

'>>>>   ON CANNERY ROW IN MONTEREY, CALIFORNIA, A SATUR-
day matinee was about to begin. In the fashion of the
Row, preparations were casual. Ten minutes before the
hour a tall young man with shaggy curls stuck his head
out an opening of the cinema, a narrow room between
an art gallery and a vacant warehouse, and spoke to the
crowd gathering on the sidewalk. "Be right with ya."

A short time later the group, about half long-haired
young adults with preadolescent children, and half long-
haired young adults unaccompanied by children, filed
into the corridor-like room and settled themselves on
the carpeted floor along the windrows of big and middle-
sized pillows which were the only furniture. The air was
heavy with incense. Rock sounded. A light show played
over the large screen, which was curved against an end
wall too narrow for a flat screen of standard size.

John Lennon sang "Imagine" and the young man
with shaggy curls moved quietly among the now mostly
supine audience, supplying extra pillows, urging them
all to get closer together so that newcomers could be
accommodated. A pillow fight broke out and was good-
humoredly put down. Just before the light show cut
off and the feature began, the young man corrected
one final problem by calling out, "You up in front,
would you please lie down so the people behind can
see?"

The picture that day was not *Flaming Creatures*,

3

nor even *The Killing of Sister George*, but MGM's thirty-three-year-old big money maker *The Wizard of Oz*, adapted from the seventy-three-year-old, all-time best selling juvenile book by L. Frank Baum. Although the screenplay has a number of laugh lines, some taken from Baum's own dialogue, as well as much added slapstick business contributed by the director and the performing comedians, the matinee audience watched the musical comedy in a silence which can only be described as a kind of half indifferent, half committed concentration. Nor was there any noticeable restiveness during the music, which includes the highly sentimental "Over the Rainbow," a song that is about as far removed as possible from the amplified rock which had shortly before been pulsing through the theater. The only real audience response—if indeed it can be called that without over-stating—came at the end of the film, when Dorothy wakes up back home in Kansas and her family tries to tell her she has had a dream. "It wasn't a dream, it's a *place*," she insists. This at last brought a small murmur and a couple of muted cheers before the curved screen went white and the stretched-out rows of bodies began to stir and rise.

The playing of *The Wizard* at a hip cinema is only one of a number of signs of the affinity for Baum and his work felt by still another generation of young people, this one the same group which in recent years has "rediscovered" Kahlil Gibran, Hermann Hesse, and the Upanishads. The new love affair between the youthful subculture and the elderly Wizard may be more serious than other such affairs, however.

And though the Saturday afternoon scene could have taken place almost anywhere in America, the fact of its happening on Cannery Row further serves to recall how the Row once dedicated itself not to fantasy in the style of Baum, but to a kind of literary naturalism peculiar to John Steinbeck. Hollow cannery shells, rusting vats, bleached skeletons of small boats, and other such detritus have been the relics which drew tourists in past times. Through the late sixties and early seventies, however, most of these leftovers from the sardine industry have disappeared with the coming of something referred to in the local press as "hip capitalism," which emphasizes crafts, underground periodicals, organic food, the communal life, and, of course, youth.

One of these new businesses, the Oz Natural Foods Restaurant, literally contains one of the older relics, a boiler from a defunct fish cannery; but its welded and riveted seams, even painted over as they are with pastel paint in psychedelic designs, somehow manage to suggest the all-metal body of the Tin Woodman in *The Wizard of Oz*.

As for how the restaurant got its name, it turns out the four young men who run it are all highly vocal devotees of the work of Baum. The lengths to which they have gone to utilize the legend of Oz seem, in fact, almost excessive. Each of the four has assumed in real life the role of an Oz character. One, a wood craftsman before losing his arm in an accident, has inevitably become the Woodman. Another lays claim to the title of Scarecrow because of a lank frame and straw-colored hair, and so on.

According to these restaurateurs, their patrons don't ask what Oz is (any more than tourists of a decade ago needed to ask who Flora was, or Sonnyboy, or Pilon). They know. Whether or not they and their counterparts elsewhere in the nation who embrace the Baum mystique will endure as an alternative society remains to be seen; but the mystique itself surely will, and right now they are its keepers.*

This is not to say that since publication of the first Oz book at the turn of the century Baum's literary and popular reputation was assured. Quite the contrary. His appeal has been a phenomenon of the giddy, off-again-on-again variety. Though he lived and wrote in California, Baum was never the favorite of the literati there that Steinbeck has been, or, to make a more appropriate comparison with a writer for young people, Robert Louis Stevenson. Nor was he ever generally extolled anywhere. Thousands of literate Americans have never heard of him, or connect his name only with a musical comedy which made financial history on Broadway in the first decade of the century, and with the durable motion picture. But the picture alone, shown regularly through the years in movie theaters and as an annual television program, can account for the visually oriented "now" generation's familiarity with Baum's most famous fairy tale.

Why the appeal of Baum's material to a subculture which has presumably rejected most antecedent ideals is another matter, and one that may run deeper than is readily apparent.

In his book *Getting Back Together*[1] Robert Houriet touches upon one major concept central both to Baum and to the disaffected young: the agrarian paradise. Typical of the groups which in the late sixties began moving to rural areas from their urban places of origin (the Haight-Ashbury neighborhood in San Francisco, the East Village in New York City) was the Oz com-

---

*Unhappily, the Oz Restaurant recently went out of business, but the youth culture still rules the Row.

mune near Meadville, Pennsylvania. Like that of Brook
Farm a century earlier, the existence of the thirty-five-
member group was ephemeral, but in the case of "Oz,"
its seed of destruction appears not to have been gener-
ated internally, at least not entirely.

Weeks of harassment by neighbors and Meadville
residents culminated in the multiple arrest of the "Ozites" for "keeping a disorderly house" under terms of a
little-used nineteenth-century Pennsylvania statute. But
during the four months of the experiment (June through
September, 1968), the group lived together in a three-
story house on a 135-acre farm, cooked outdoors,
bathed in a nearby stream, and worked for neighboring
farmers—those few who remained reasonably friendly—
in exchange for produce rather than money.

Unlike many of their peers, these commune members were said to be less interested in drugs than in the
kind of "natural high" that comes of eating indigenous
food and living "the good life." In their rejection of
urban values—including avoidance of modish dress, elim-
ination of interpersonal competition, and substitution
of a barter system for money—they managed to remain,
during their brief shared life, true to their name.

The Wonderful Wizard of Oz (the original title of
the book which came out in 1900) first introduced
Americans to Baum's lush, pastoral fairyland where good
inevitably triumphs over evil by the power of love, not
war. There is a city in the land, ruled by a wizard, and
while the main characters feel impelled to journey to
this city to have their needs satisfied, it turns out that
at the heart of the urban society there is fraud and
deceit, that the wizard is a humbug, that their hope of
salvation lies in their own internal resources as opposed
to external assistance. Though they do, in a manner of

speaking, get what they came for, because they insist on it, it is abundantly clear that what they receive is to be taken by the reader as only the outward and visible sign of an inner state which already existed.

Later, when Baum's vision of Oz was extended into a series, the Emerald City becomes a more benign setting, but no doubt remains about the original point. "There's a freedom and independence in country life that not even the Emerald City can give one."[2]

And in 1903, when Baum was still in the period in which most critics agree he did his best writing, a more conventional fairy tale, *The Enchanted Island of Yew*, was published. Compared with Oz, Yew is an inferior fairyland, but the book contains a passage which could well serve as the preamble to a manifesto for today's green revolution:

> In the old days, when the world was young, there were no automobiles nor flying-machines to make one wonder; nor were there railway trains, nor telephones, nor mechanical inventions of any sort to keep people keyed up to a high pitch of excitement. Men and women lived simply and quietly. They were Nature's children, and breathed fresh air into their lungs instead of smoke and coal gas; and tramped through green meadows and deep forests instead of riding in street cars; and went to bed when it grew dark and rose with the sun—which is vastly different from the present custom.[3]

Baum goes on here to give his theory of the fairy tale and to reproach his own age for having left no room for fantasy in its preoccupation with progress.

Charles A. Reich, in his survey of the youth culture, says:

> The great question of these times is how to live in and with a technological society; what mind and what way of life can preserve man's humanity and his very existence against the domination of the forces he has created. This question is at the root of the American crisis, beneath all the immediate issues of lawlessness, poverty, meaninglessness, and war. It is this question to which America's new generation is beginning to discover an answer, an answer based on a renewal of life that carries hope of restoring us to our sources and ourselves.[4]

It might be added that it is not only the retreat to the simpler life, but the commune-as-living-arrangement itself which is a point of contingence between Baum and the counterculture. Gerald Dworkin explains:

> Another fairly important development, still in too early a stage to be assessed fully, is what the sociologists would call the 'breakdown of the nuclear family and a return to the extended family.' What this means in English is that the typical Hippie household is not two parents and 2.5 children, but rather a heterogeneous grouping of six or eight people, some of them, perhaps, being children linked to each other by ties which are in many ways family-like.[5]

Like most other protagonists of juvenile literature, Baum's principal characters rarely have parents, and never a complete set. Dorothy is an orphan, living with her aunt and uncle. Trot's mother is mentioned in passing when Trot first appears, in a fairy tale out of the Oz cycle (*The Sea Fairies*), but forgotten when Trot comes to live in Oz. Button Bright makes his appearance (*The Road to Oz*) in an unexplained parentless state, and remains so. And of those characters whose origins are in fairyland, such a generalization can be made even more emphatic. Either they are manufactured, like the Scarecrow, or they are orphans, like Tip (*The Land of Oz*), whose custodian is a witch, or Ojo (*The Patchwork Girl of Oz*), who lives with an uncle.

The movement toward communal life comes for many of the protagonists of the various books as the series progresses and one by one they take up residence in Oz at the invitation of the Princess Ozma, most of them becoming members of the "extended family" at the palace itself. Even Dorothy's aunt and uncle join the group eventually, as a solution to the imminent mortgage foreclosure back home on the Kansas farm.

Joining the commune, however, is in no sense a mergence either for the youthful member of the counterculture or for the Ozite. On the contrary. The insistence on the worth of the individual, including the idea that eccentricity is an indication of merit, is a theme that is sounded in the first Oz story and carried through to the end, both in the fourteen Oz books and in Baum's other writing. It provides not only a moral principle but serves as a structural device in that the stories—looked at from this point of view at least—are simply the introduction of the reader to increasingly strange characters with a wide assortment of qualities and capacities whose fortunes are then pursued throughout the book as they undertake a complicated journey to achieve some worthy goal.

The tin man and the Scarecrow of the first story are joined by a stick man with a pumpkin head, a live sawhorse, and a gigantic talking beetle (anticipating Kafka) in the second (*The Land of Oz*). Other eccentrics in and out of Oz include an animated gingerbread man (hardly an original idea with Baum, though he adds some interesting refinements), a glass cat, a "girl" made of a rolled-up patchwork quilt, a "man" made of copper who thinks and acts by clockwork, and many more.

All are entirely acceptable to, and accepted by, the other characters, the idiosyncrasies represented usually being regarded as valuable, even endearing, qualities once one has embraced the not really contradictory notion of oddness as a norm.

> 'But—pardon me if I seem inquisitive—are you not all rather—ahem!—rather unusual?' asked the Woggle-Bug, looking from one to another with unconcealed interest.
>
> 'No more so than yourself,' answered the Scarecrow. 'Everything in life is unusual until you get accustomed to it.'[6]

In fact so enthusiastic does the author become in his long enumeration of virtuous idiosyncrasies, that the description of Tik-Tok the copper man seems to condone, in a curious paraphrase of Ecclesiastes, the very item earlier anathematized, the machine:

> Perhaps it is better to be a machine that does

its duty than a flesh-and-blood person who will not, for a dead truth is better than a live falsehood.[7]

(True, Baum has previously made it clear that Tik-Tok "thinks, speaks, acts, and *does everything but live*,"[8] so the superiority of the machine is considerably qualified.)

It is probably inevitable, if the idea of exalted individuality is carried far enough, that a note of snobbery will be struck sooner or later. Even the Oz characters are not immune. The Scarecrow remarks:

'. . . I am convinced that the only people worthy of consideration in this world are the unusual ones. For the common folks are like the leaves of a tree, and live and die unnoticed.'[9]

As the series continues, the original idea of self worth is actually eroded by this emphasis on exclusiveness. In *The Lost Princess of Oz*, the eleventh of the fourteen Oz books, two reiterations appear, one by the Cowardly Lion:

'. . . were you all like me, I would çonsider you so common that I would not care to associate with you. To be individual, my friends, to be different from others, is the only way to become distinguished from the common herd.'[10]

And another by Scraps, the Patchwork Girl:

bors will envy you, and for that reason both civilized foxes and civilized humans spend most of their time dressing themselves.'

'I don't,' said the shaggy man.

'That is true,' said the King, looking at him carefully; 'but perhaps you are not civilized.'[16]

Earlier, in preparation for a banquet given by the foxes, Dorothy has consented to having ribbons pinned to her shoulders as a polite concession to fox values, but "when they met the shaggy man in the splendid drawing-room of the palace they found him just the same as before. He had refused to give up his shaggy clothes for new ones, because if he did that he would no longer be the shaggy man, he said. . . ."[17]

When the party arrives in the Emerald City, however, it discovers that Ozma has prepared new festive garb for all the visitors. For the Shaggy Man there is an elegant suit of clothing and "everything about it was shaggy . . . and he sighed with contentment to realize that he could now be finely dressed and still be the Shaggy Man. His coat was of rose-colored velvet, trimmed with shags and bobtails, with buttons of blood-red rubies and golden shags around the edges. . . ."[18]

Of course, the "success" of this kind of individuality depends upon acceptance by a group rather than solitary existence. In addition to the preference for communal arrangements already mentioned, there is an emphasis, both in Oz and in the alternative society, on group experience. Whether or not the group is casual and fluid, or relatively stable (as in the commune) does not matter in this case. Reich says the new culture "rests on two integrated concepts: respect for the

'Right or wrong . . . to be different is to be distinguished. . . . Now, in my case, I'm just like all other patchwork girls because I'm the only one there is.'[11]

According to Reich, strong emphasis on individuality (if not its refinement into snobbery) is a basic article of faith among today's young people, whose thinking "postulates the absolute worth of every human being—every self."[12]

People are brothers, the world is ample for all. . . . A boy who was odd in some way used to suffer derision all through his school days. Today there would be no persecution; one might even hear one boy speak, with affection, of 'my freaky friend.' Instead of insisting that everyone be measured by given standards, the new generation values what is unique and different in each self; there is no pressure that anyone be an athlete unless he wants to; a harpsichord player is accepted on equal terms. No one judges anyone else.

This assessment is plainly ingenuous, for there *are* limits to the kinds of idiosyncrasy acceptable in the new society, as anyone who has had first-hand experience with the "now" people would agree. A nonsmoker in a room where joints are being passed is about as comfortable as an AA member at a drunken brawl. And a student of mine, a member of the subculture until he was drafted and made an MP, claimed the worst moment of his life was having to walk, shorthaired and in uniform, across a campus quadrangle filled with a noontime crowd of his peers, all longhaired, beaded, bearded, and face-painted. For it is only reasonable (and human) that a life style which encourages south by southwesterly eccentricity cannot accommodate an eccentric whose bent is north by northeast.

But then Baum had his limits too. When Zeb, Dorothy, and the Wizard meet the braided man inside Pyramid Mountain (*Dorothy and the Wizard in Oz*), he tells them his story. He is an inventor who manufactures flutters for flags and rustles for ladies' silk gowns. On earth he had manufactured imported holes for American Swiss cheese, pores for porous plaster, and holes for doughnuts and buttons, and had invented an adjustable post-hole. But this last item was, quite literally, his downfall; having little storage space, he began stacking the post-holes end to end, making an extraordinarily long hole. When he leaned over it to try to see bottom, he lost his balance and tumbled into the earth, landing near the underground mountain, where he decided to stay, and where the Ozites find him.

> When the braided man had completed this strange tale Dorothy nearly laughed, because it was all so absurd; but the Wizard tapped his forehead significantly, to indicate that he thought the poor man was crazy.[13]

It is never made clear by what standards the braided man is judged insane, while other Oz characters whose experiences seem no less outrageously whimsical are sane. A case in point is of course the Tin Woodman, once a man of flesh and blood who while chopping wood has cut off, seriatim, his arms, legs, head, and trunk with his ax, and has had these items replaced, one

by one, by a tinsmith, until ⬚⬚⬚⬚ wholly of metal.

But no discussion of individuali⬚⬚ plete without mention of attitudes to⬚ Reich calls the clothing of the counterc⬚ tremely expressive of the human body, and ea⬚ is different and unique. . . . If the individual w⬚ he can add touches to his clothes that make them costume, expressing whatever he feels at the moment."[14]

In Baum, descriptions of fantastic clothing abound. Jack Pumpkinhead at his creation is dressed in purple trousers, red shirt, and pink vest dotted with white. Lavish descriptions are used in connection with the costumes worn at Ozma's palace. Even the Tin Woodman, precluded from wearing clothing for reasons never given, causes himself to be nickel-plated and polished with putz-pomade after he develops a case of vanity between the first book and the second.[15]

However, Baum, like the youth culture, draws the fine distinction between clothing for style value (which implies uniformity) and clothing as self-expression. The Shaggy Man, for instance, a long-hair freak in anybody's milieu, is explicit on this point (*The Road to Oz*). When Dorothy's party arrives in Foxville and inquires of the fox king why his subjects don't wear their own hairy skins, since foxes are born without clothes, the following conversation occurs:

> 'So were human beings born without clothes,' he [the king] replied; 'and until they became civilized they wore only their natural skins. But to become civilized means to dress as elaborately and prettily as possible, and to make a show of your clothes so your neigh-

uniqueness of each individual, and the idea expressed by the word 'together'."[19]

Baum's eccentrics never set out upon their quests alone, nor does the circle ever close, the original company of two or three usually expanding along the way. The Lonesome Duck, who "can't make friends because everyone I meet—bird, beast or person—is disagreeable to me,"[20] represents aberration in the Land of Oz. Although the Duck has a palace of diamonds, Dorothy muses: ". . . but if you live in it all alone, I don't see why it's any better than a wooden palace. . . ."[21]

Throughout the Oz series, talents which arise from the unique capacities of the individuals are directed to the preservation and enrichment of the group. In *The Scarecrow of Oz* only the Ork can save the group by flying over the black chasm; in *The Tin Woodman of Oz* only the Scarecrow can provide the Hip-po-gy-raf with the straw he demands for ferrying the group over the impassable ditch because his (the Scarecrow's) body is stuffed with it, so he allows himself to be unstuffed and sacrificed.

But no one of them, it seems, understands the concept of solidarity of the heterogeneous group better than the Shaggy Man, who declares: ". . . I never criticize my friends. If they are really true friends, they may be anything they like, for all of me."[22]

It is the Shaggy Man again who best serves to emphasize that in Oz love is the universal solvent. Not only does it remove obstacles and disarm enemies, it serves as currency. The Shaggy Man carries an amulet called the Love Magnet, an explanation of the function of which would seem supererogatory.

'Money,' declared the shaggy man, 'makes

people proud and haughty; I don't want to be proud and haughty. All I want is to have people love me; and as long as I own the Love Magnet everyone I meet is sure to love me dearly.'[23]

But the magnet proves useless when he reaches Oz, where, as Ozma explains, "we are loved for ourselves alone, and for our kindness to one another. . . ."[24] And since he can't even give the magnet away, it is hung over the gate to the Emerald City and restored to the Shaggy Man only on the occasions of his subsequent adventures *outside* the Land of Oz.

Money has already been listed as one of the devices of the urban society which is to be rejected along with that society. And next to the destruction of flags and draft cards, perhaps no demonstration by youthful dropouts has made more of an impression upon the established society than the occasional blazing piles of currency on Wall Street and elsewhere.

It almost goes without saying that no traveler in Oz would expect to have to use money there. It is perhaps for this reason that Baum's few lapses on the subject— he apparently had a bit of trouble getting used to the idea himself—are quite noticeable. In *The Wizard* Dorothy observes children in the Emerald City buying green lemonade with green pennies,[25] but that was in the time when the fraudulent wizard was still in charge and the urban setting full of corruption. In *The Land of Oz* a ferryman offers to row Tip and Jack across a stream "if you have money."[26] Yet in the same book the jackdaw's nest, outside of Oz, is full of paper currency which is considered valuable by the Oz group only as new stuffing for the Scarecrow. And in *The Road to*

Oz this dialogue is recorded:

> 'Money! Money in Oz!' cried the Tin Wood-
> man. 'What a queer idea! Did you suppose
> we are so vulgar as to use money here?'
>
> 'Why not?' asked the shaggy man.
>
> 'If we used money to buy things with, instead
> of love and kindness and the desire to please
> one another, then we should be no better than
> the rest of the world,' declared the Tin Wood-
> man. 'Fortunately money is not known in the
> Land of Oz at all. We have no rich, and no
> poor; for what one wishes the others all try to
> give him, in order to make him happy, and no
> one in all Oz cares to have more than he can
> use.'[27]

The Shaggy Man is thus defeated at his own game.
Having come from the real world, where his views of
love and money are the exception, he decides to remain
permanently in Oz, where he is "at home" because these
same exceptional ideals are already the norm. If the
Shaggy Man is at least partially representative, as seems
likely, of Baum's acknowledgement of the conditions
among the American unemployed which culminated
in Coxey's Army in the author's own time, then this is
indeed the story of the hobo who finally does reach the
Big Rock Candy Mountains by rejecting capitalism entirely.

When Dorothy first finds Shaggy wandering down
a Kansas road he is obviously a tramp on the dole. He
does not work. But in Joe Hill's ballad, the proper
answer to the establishment question, "Oh, why don't

you work, like other men do?" is, "How the hell can I work when there's no work to do?"[28]

It has been often enough remarked by detractors of the hip culture that it could exist only in an economy wealthy enough to support it by way of the parental remittance and the welfare subsidy. Reich, however, while not disputing this point, attacks the subject from a slightly different perspective. Poverty and unemployment are flaws in the corporate state, and the alternative society's answer to these particular problems is the same as its answer to all the others: rejection of the state itself. Thus a misconception has arisen that today's young people are unwilling to work.

> The new generation is not 'lazy,' and it is glad enough to put great effort into any work that is worthwhile, whether it is hours of practice on a musical instrument, or working on a communal farm, or helping to create People's Park in Berkeley. But they see industrialized work as one of the chief means by which the minds and feelings of people are dominated in the Corporate State.[29]

Also in Oz, where everyone works only half the time and plays the other half, work is always meaningful. One performs at whatever one does best: farming, shoemaking, tailoring, jewelry making. The results are distributed according to need. This system at once solves the problem of the organization man who can see no useful product which he can truly call a result of his own effort, and the frustrated and deceived consumer manipulated from "above." As the Shaggy Man discovered, in Oz the alternative system is already functioning with success.

Still another phenomenon arising from the mentioned total rather than selective rejection of the established society is the renunciation by the counterculture not only of things academic but those intellectual. This is of course contrary to other anti-establishment movements in American history, but hardly surprising in a generation which values the "felt," or sensuous, experience over the intellectualized one.

If the core of the youth culture is indeed the very cream of society, the sons and daughters of upper middleclass families well above average in intelligence and educational opportunity, it is also a group known to have "deep skepticism of both 'linear' and analytic thought,"[30] a skepticism brought about by the failure of this kind of reasoning to solve the quandaries the country now faces. Reich contends that this bias, combined with the breakdown of what younger people consider the false values of their elders, is manifested, among other ways, in the fact that: "Students a few years ago were keenly aware of whether they were being taught by an assistant professor or an associate professor. Students today have no idea at all of their teachers' rank. They do not see it because it is not there."[31]

In Oz a broad satire of the academic begins with the Woggle-Bug, a pompous caricature of every pretentious bore who ever annoyed Baum in real life, and cuts in many directions. T. E. Woggle-Bug, H. M. (the initials standing for "thoroughly educated" and "highly magnified") was once an ordinary bug living in a floor crack in a schoolroom. After being exposed to professorial lectures daily over a long period, the bug is discovered and picked up by the instructor, who during a science lesson puts his captive on a microscope slide and

projects him onto a screen. The bug manages to escape
in this "highly magnified" condition, hence his enormous size when the Ozites meet him (*Land of Oz*).
Later in the series (*The Emerald City*) Professor Woggle-
Bug has become director of The Royal Athletic College
of Oz and has developed a scheme for instant education.

> 'These are the Algebra Pills,' said the Profes-
> sor, taking down one of the bottles. 'One at
> night, on retiring, is equal to four hours of
> study. Here are the Geography Pills—one at
> night and one in the morning. In this next
> bottle are the Latin Pills—one three times a
> day . . . they are sugarcoated and easily
> swallowed. I believe the students would rather
> take the pills than study. . . . You see, until
> these School Pills were invented we wasted a
> lot of time in study that may now be better
> employed in practising athletics.'[32]

The Woggle-Bug's image is faintly reflected later in
the Oz cycle with the Frogman, who like the Wizard is a
humbug, but unlike the Wizard (and like the Woggle-
Bug himself) is self-deluded. "I shall probably astonish
strangers, because they have never before had the pleas-
ure of seeing me. Also they will marvel at my great
learning. Every time I open my mouth, Cayke, I am
liable to say something important," he tells Cayke the
Cookie Cook in *The Lost Princess*.[33]

A more direct thrust at academe comes with the
description of the Rigmaroles (*The Emerald City*),
whose speech is so convoluted as to be totally incomprehensible, and who are compared by the Shaggy Man to
college lecturers and ministers. And it is the Sea Serpent

(*The Sea Fairies*) who remarks: "People who are always understood are very common. You are sure to respect those you can't understand, for you feel that perhaps they know more than you do."[34]   This kind of thing is well within the long tradition of anti-intellectualism which has also produced, among other things, Oscar Wilde's "I live in continual fear of not being misunderstood," and W. S. Gilbert's " 'A fool is bent upon a twig, but wise men dread a bandit.'/Which I think must have been clever, for I didn't understand it."[35]

But Baum, far from stopping here, shows his prejudice extends to music as well. In an exchange between Tietjamus Toips, the composer (*John Dough and the Cherub*), and the gingerbread man, the latter pronounces a composition "awful discord." But Toips assures him that "such praise gladdens my heart and makes me very happy! Ah! glorious moment, in which I produce music that is not understood and sounds like discord!"[36] In a later book (*The Patchwork Girl*) a phonograph, accidentally animated when some of the Powder of Life is spilled over it, pursues the protagonal group playing its records. When the group objects to the noise, the machine, which is personified to the point of being given a name, Victor Columbia Edison, tells them:

> 'It is classical music, and is considered the best
> and most puzzling ever manufactured. You're
> supposed to like it, whether you do or not,
> and if you don't the proper thing is to look as
> if you did. . . .'[37]

And yet the true basis of affinity between Baum and the counterculture on this point is far more firmly rooted than in such surface statements of anti-intellect-

ualism (if that is really the word for Baum's bias; this is
a matter to be taken up again in a later section). In his
very act of becoming a writer of the fairy tale, a vener-
able and important form of romance, Baum has staked
claim to the two major organizing elements of the genre:
magic and innocence. In turning away from nineteenth-century rationalism, he has anticipated an even
more emphatic turning away from rationalism in our
own time. Reich lists as important to the new order:

> . . . a desire for innocence, for the ability to
> be in a state of wonder or awe. It is of the
> essence of the thinking of the new generation
> that man should be constantly open to new
> experience, constantly ready to have his old
> ways of thinking changed, constantly hoping
> that he will be sensitive enough and receptive
> enough to let the wonders of nature and man-
> kind come to him.[38]

Baum's own pleas for this return to a state of innocence and wonder are many. The Shaggy Man tells
Betsy Bobbin:

> 'All the magic isn't in fairyland. . . . There's
> lots of magic in all Nature, and you may see it
> as well in the United States, where you and I
> once lived, as you can here.'[39]

The inevitable corollary idea here, that of retreat
to somewhere "other," transcending normal experience
by whatever device, is certainly more a predisposition
which involves the whole human race rather than the
peculiar notion of a single generation. Yet surely no

generation anywhere, at any time, has placed more
unselfconscious emphasis on "tripping" than this one.

Drugs, music, and other sense experiences, including nonverbal touch encounters, incense, and lighting
effects—all are aimed toward the goal of breaking down
the wall between "normal" perception and whatever
lies "beyond." Speaking of the youth culture and its
experience with LSD, Mark Harris says:

> For many, it precipitated gorgeous hallucina-
> tions, a wide variety of sensual perceptions
> never before available to the user, and breath-
> taking panoramic visions of human and social
> perfection accompanied by profound insights
> into the user's own past.[40]

Whether the journey to Oz or one of the other
Baumian fairylands is conceived of as a mental or
spatial trip matters very little in this context. The
author does make it clear, by the simple expedient of
furnishing a map, that these lands all exist on the same
continent (the continent of his own imagination?) which
lies in the Nonestic Ocean. (With a smattering of classics
himself, he would have expected the young readers of
his own time to know Latin for "it is not.") The title
The Enchanted Island of Yew also suggests that Baum
conceived of the fairy country as existing in Yew (You),
or in the individual imagination. But not, of course, in
the cold, aseptic, unturned-on confines of the rational
imagination. Writer Miriam Allen DeFord has done us
the favor of pointing out what vastness lies between the
Latin meanings of *hinc* and *illinc*.[41] In a world which
can be divided by general agreement into "this side"
and "the other side," Oz is obviously to be found in the

latter.

But perhaps the most obvious of all links between Baum and the new generation is the concept of absolute pacifism. Harris reminds us of

> . . . the hippies' unwavering adherence to the ideal of nonviolence. Miraculously, they retained it in a community and in a world whose easiest tendency was guns. For that virtue, if for no other, they valuably challenged American life. If they did not oppose the war in Vietnam in the way of organized groups, they opposed it by the argument of example, avoiding violence under all circumstances. They owned no guns.[42]

In early 1969 the Army conducted mutiny courts martial at Fort Ord, California, which centered on the shooting death of a young AWOL soldier at the San Francisco Presidio Stockade the previous fall. The defendants at these trials, all around twenty years old, most of them school dropouts, had in the spirit of the times defied authority, and were certainly considerable as part of the general disaffection with militarism.

Interestingly, the nickname they had given the dead youth, who was quite small physically, was "Munchkin."

Their choice of a literary reference from Baum was perhaps not so conscious as in the case of the Oz commune members, who, according to Houriet, actually conducted readings from the "sacred texts" (the Oz books), but it was nonetheless singularly appropriate. One of the durable running jokes in the series concerns the Army of Oz, which has twenty-seven officers and one private, the last to do the fighting. But Ozma, the girl ruler, believes all problems can be settled without fighting, so the private is made a captain-general. With no one left to do battle, no battle is done. It is precisely this line of reasoning which is so often used by today's pacifists as an argument for demobilizing all armies and destroying all weapons.

Furthermore, the slogan of the organization called Mothers and Others for Peace, "War is not healthy for children and other living things," could easily be a paraphrase of Baum's much-quoted axiom, "Fighting is unkind and liable to be injurious to others."[43]

The fullest statement of the Ozian position, however, is made by Princess Ozma herself just before the invasion of the Land of Oz by a horde of dangerous enemies:

> '. . . I do not wish to fight. . . . No one has the right to destroy any living creatures, however evil they may be, or to hurt them or make them unhappy. I will not fight—even to save my kingdom. . . . Because the Nome King intends to do evil is no excuse for my doing the same.'[44]

And if Ozma's insistence on unilateral demobilization is Baum's answer to war, the situation of the "scattered" general in *John Dough* may well be his specific criticism of United States involvement in foreign wars, a comment with particularly audible echoes today.

The general, "hero of a hundred battles," including Waterloo, is accused by the king of being scattered all over the world because he was "foolish." His head is now made of wax; one leg is cork, the other basswood; his arms are rubber. He answers the king:

'To an extent, Sire, I am scattered. But it is the result of bravery, not foolishness.' He unstrapped his left arm and tossed it on the floor before the throne. 'I lost that at Bull Run,' he said. Then he unhooked his right leg and cast it down. 'That, Sire, was blown off at Sedan.' Then he suddenly lifted his right arm, seized his hair firmly, and lifted the head from his shoulders. 'It is true I lost my head at Santiago,' he said, 'but I could not help it.'[45]

So strong is the anti-war sentiment in the Land of Oz and the peripheral fairylands, in fact, that this item alone might be enough to insure Baum's place among the counter-establishment of today.

★　★　★　★　★

To investigate Baum's influence in the "now" world, however, is to tell only half the story, perhaps less than half. The unevenness of his critical reputation has already been mentioned, but despite this handicap, Oz has relentlessly permeated American culture.

For one thing, the very word "Oz" has entered both the spoken and written language (though evidently not yet the dictionary) to mean any imaginary place, or to evoke an aura of the exotic or the sumptuous, in the manner of the land of cockaigne of medieval literature. But more telling still, references requiring thorough familiarity with Baum characters and incidents turn up frequently in writing from the most casual to

the most formal.[46]   Or if not this, a writer assuming
ignorance of Oz on the part of his readers will take the
most strenuous care to set them right. Helen McNeil,
for instance, begins a book review in the New Statesman:

> In *The Wizard of Oz*, a Kansas cyclone carries
> away Dorothy's farmhouse and drops it in the
> magical land of Oz; patterned on the Middle
> West, Oz is an enormous square, divided by a
> crossroads into four coloured quadrants with
> four proprietary witches representing the four
> points of the compass, who initiate 'Dorothy
> from Kansas' into their ways of absolute good
> and evil. Oz is bounded on all sides by the
> impassable Deadly Desert. Dorothy has many
> adventures and never comes home again.[47]

Miss McNeil's glimpse of Oz is clouded, as any Baum
cultist would know. Oz is not a square, but a rectangle,
its length about half again the size of its width, and the
Yellow Brick Road, far from forming a neat crossroads
at the geographic center of Oz, meanders north-north-
west from the eastern border in the Munchkin Country,
to the Emerald City, where it stops. Another road goes
straight south to Glinda's palace in the Quadling country, but aside from these, roads are unreliable in Oz, a
contributary complication in the adventures of Dorothy
in *The Wizard* when she goes to seek the Wicked Witch
of the West, as well as in subsequent adventures in succeeding books. It is true Dorothy is told there were
once four witches. But by the time she sets foot in Oz,
her house has already demolished one of the wicked
ones. She meets both the good ones, and "melts" the
second wicked one with water. Another bad witch,

Mombi, pops up in the very next book, *The Land of Oz*, but this has nothing to do with Dorothy, who has by then returned to Kansas, contrary to Miss McNeil's assertion that she "never goes home again."

Yet the point is not that a reviewer for the *New Statesman* should be confused about Oz, a confusion she shares with many writers, including Baum himself, whose numerous contradictions of "fact" about the Land of Oz throughout the series are well known to aficionados. Rather the significance lies in so much space being given to trying to acquaint a sophisticated British readership with the intricacies of Oz.

On the commercial front, too, it is inevitable that Oz should become (or remain) a useful label. A check through telephone directories of major American cities shows Oz food stores, gift shops, and novelty makers. A Land of Oz Park opened in June, 1970, near Banner Elk, North Carolina, probably providing the inspiration for a *Chicago Tribune* cartoon in which a man in an airfield tower announces: "Flight 47 to Disneyland has been hijacked to the Land of Oz."[48]

One of Baum's biographers has noted that the National Radio Astronomy laboratory at Green Bank, West Virginia, keeps a vigil for possible signals from intelligent beings in outer space and calls it Project OZMA.[49] In Chicago, where Baum once lived, there is an L. Frank Baum (elementary) school.

Yet until the mid-nineteen-fifties, and despite the fact that over the years *The Wizard* was consistently outselling any other children's book, practically no "serious" notice was taken of Baum.

There are exceptions. In 1929 Edward Wagenknecht published an appreciation[50] of Baum which took note of his appeal as a satirist and social critic as well as a writer for children. And in 1934 James Thurber wrote a brief essay for the *New Republic* in which he indicated his own nostalgic preference for the earlier books in the Oz series over the later ones.[51]

Scattered instances of publicity in the popular press, however, had to do mostly with the 1939 film. A review of this movie, again in the *New Statesman*, paid Baum this doubtful compliment: *"Oz* is as common to American homes as *Mein Kampf* is in German."[52]

The year 1956, however, marked the beginning of a minor Ozian renaissance, the result of the coinciding of several events.   For one thing it was the Baum centenary (he was born May 15, 1856), and Roland Baughman, curator of special collections at Columbia University's Butler Library, planned and presented the most nearly complete display of Baum's work possible at that time. It also happened to be the year *The Wizard* became public domain. A number of publishers added the book to their lists, and this in turn fanned to white heat the long-smoldering embers of the old feud, when book critics and children's librarians saw the lists and were reminded again of Baum, whom they had been trying to ignore, if not suppress.

Out of this same period came two quite serious essays on Baum by Martin Gardner and Russel B. Nye,[53] published together in 1957 as *The Wizard of Oz and Who He Was.*[54]   The volume includes a partially anno-tated edition of the *Wizard*, as well as the first attempt at a comprehensive bibliography covering the volumi-nous pseudonymous writings of Baum, along with those better known.

And finally, that watershed season of 1956-57 also saw the founding of the International Wizard of Oz Club, Inc.   In past times several publisher-sponsored

Baum fan clubs for children had flourished with varying degrees of endurance, but the new group was the first to attract large numbers of adults who had read Baum as children and retained their appreciation.

Quite apart from all this critical and official attention, however, the Oz books marched on, captivating new waves of young readers every year, while holding onto a special place in the affections of the adults which these readers became. No one, it seems, had difficulty understanding the references in Ray Bradbury's short story "The Exiles,"[55] set in the year 2120, which assumed that to escape a civilization of zealous hyper-rationalists, the Emerald City has moved to Mars, along with all the fantasy and magic which has previously been the heritage of the human race. But the enemy arrives to take over Mars too and all is lost. The tale ends with the tossing of the last Oz book in existence onto the pyre of destruction while the Emerald City crumbles into ruin in the background. And this story came out in 1950, well before the renewed interest in Oz and its author.

Since the fifties there has been a (comparative) proliferation of material on Baum, most of it enthusiastic, some of it very worthwhile indeed. In the latter category is Henry M. Littlefield's thoughtful "The Wizard of Oz: Parable on Populism,"[56] in which the Tin Woodman is seen as the eastern industrial worker (he is discovered by Dorothy in the eastern land of the Munchkins), the Scarecrow as the farmer, and the Lion as the politician (William Jennings Bryan), who as a group approach the Wizard (McKinley) to ask for relief from their sufferings. Dorothy's magical silver shoes (the proposed silver standard) traveling along the Yellow Brick Road (gold) are lost forever in the Deadly Desert when she returns to Kansas (when Bryan lost the election).

One of the major efforts on Baum's behalf in these latter days has been the 1961 publication of *To Please a Child*, a biography done partially as a memoir by a son, Frank Joslyn Baum, in collaboration with Russell P. MacFall.[57]

If there is anything these recent writers about Baum are likely to agree wholeheartedly upon, it is that there is far more to the story of Oz than a fairy tale for children, while on the other hand, if the work *is* viewed as children's literature, Baum has few (maybe no) peers.

By now the *Wizard* has sold from five to nine million copies[58] and since 1956 has been available in at least twenty editions from almost as many publishers, and this figure does not include non-English editions. Among other places, Oz is celebrated in Russia; some curious liberties taken in translating and interpreting the text for a Russian readership, however, make it a slightly different Oz from that known to the rest of the world.[59]

Wide differentials between popularity of a book and its literary merit are of course commonplace, especially in a country where sales depend far less on reviewer judgment than on volume of advertising, book club, film, and paperback contracts, and wild luck. Baum's case is curious, however, if only for the marked show of passion on the part of both attackers and defenders.

As one of those who reacted to the centenary flurry over Baum, Ralph Ulveling, director of libraries for the city of Detroit, in 1957 announced that *The Wizard* would be tolerated in the stacks but not in either the children's room or at the branch libraries in his system.   He told a library conference in Lansing that the Oz books are guilty of negativism, "have a cowardly approach to life," and added that "there is nothing uplifting or elevating about the Baum series."[60]   A similar indictment came the following year when the · state librarian of Florida included Oz on a list of books which she urged all public libraries to withdraw on grounds they were "poorly written, untrue to life, sensational, foolishly sentimental and consequently unwholesome. . . ."[61]

And at about this same time Dr. Frank B. Sessa, chairman of the Miami (Florida) Public Library, endeared himself forever to Baum's fellow-pacifists by declaring: "Kids don't like that fanciful stuff anymore. They want books about missiles and atomic submarines."[62]

But perhaps the unkindest cut came from Clifton Fadiman, who in 1958 published his list of "fifty best children's books," and omitted *The Wizard*.

As recently as May, 1969, according to Ann E. Prentice, writing as a doctoral candidate in library science at Columbia University, a survey of card catalogues around New York state (Baum's birthplace) turned up Baum commentary and biography but no Oz books. When librarians there were pressed to explain why, they said Oz books are "not on recommended lists," and Mrs. Prentice indeed goes on to cite a number of these lists on which Oz books do not appear.[63]

From this evidence it would seem that the note of euphoric optimism struck by Martin Gardner in his capacity as new chairman of the IWOC back in 1957 was premature:

For half a century the self-magnified, badly
educated woggle-bugs who run our public
libraries and write books about children's literature have been afraid to praise the Oz
books. (How could anything so popular, they
say to themselves, be anything but trash? Of
course it never occurs to them to *read* an Oz
book and decide for themselves.) But now,
for the first time, Oz fans are beginning to cry
out against this conspiracy of silence and to
say, without being in the least ashamed, that
the Royal History is a great and enduring work
of American literature.[64]

It may certainly be said for the IWOC that its
members are thoroughly committed to Baum and pro-
foundly determined to perpetuate the Oz mythology.
Its founder was Justin G. Schiller, who at the time
(1957) was a twelve-year-old Oz collector; he is now a
rare-book dealer in Brooklyn. From the first, membership has shown a high percentage of teachers, writers,
doctors, housewives, and other proponents of the establishment, as well as serious collectors of Americana. The
official publication, a thrice-yearly offset magazine
called the *Baum Bugle*, regularly carries descriptive data
for bibliophiles, critical and research articles by club
members, memoirs by Baum descendants, illustrations
and information on Baumiana, and related material.
A membership figure of nearly one thousand was
announced in the summer of 1973 by the international
secretary, Fred Meyer, of Escanaba, Michigan.
    Like its prototype, the Baker Street Irregulars, the
organization holds conventions and theoretical discus-
sions, the latter on such topics as why Jim the Cabhorse

caused such a sensation in Oz on grounds he was the first horse ever seen there, while Tip, who had never been out of Oz, seemed to know all about horses when he brought the sawhorse to life four books earlier. And why the powder of life, kept in a pepper box, didn't animate the pepper box.

If the IWOC has a weakness, it may lie in an apparent predisposition to embrace with almost equal fervor all that has been written about Oz by other writers than Baum, and to sing praises of Baum's prolific but less valuable writings with as much zeal as is shown toward his more successful (from an artistic viewpoint) material. For in addition to his fourteen Oz books, Baum wrote at least fifty-five other juvenile and adult books, some of them using the *noms de plume*: Schuyler Staunton, Laura Bancroft, Edith Van Dyne, Suzanne (Susanne) Metcalfe, John Estes Cook, Floyd Akers, and Captain Hugh Fitzgerald. Since his death in 1919, the Oz series has been carried on by at least seven other writers, including Ruth Plumly Thompson, who wrote nineteen books about Oz, five more than Baum himself; illustrator John R. Neill, who wrote three; Jack Snow, who wrote two, and Rachel Cosgrove, Eloise McGraw, Lauren Wagner, and Frank Joslyn Baum, who wrote one each.

But to make some final comments on the lengthy Baum controversy, it would seem currently that while the library-school anti-Oz alliance is still presenting a united and forbidding front officially, it has already yielded in every important way unofficially. An article in the *English-Speaking Forum*, a publication circulating to teachers of English in countries outside continental United States, emphasizes that *The Wizard* appears in a dozen foreign languages and is now being used to teach English as a second language in India as well as Russia.[65]

Schools and teachers have also for some time lent tacit approval to Baum with their innumerable PTA carnivals and other school events using Oz themes. Some of these are almost incredibly elaborate, as parents of elementary scholars discover. At secondary level, *The Wizard* is often given as a play, or—perhaps more often— the general plot structure, solidly familiar to both players and audience, is used freely as the basis for ad lib farce, or even for a "happening." Elsewhere on the education scene a teacher specializing in trying to "reach" psychologically disturbed adolescents and young adults says she has discovered the two writers who seem always to get a response in her classes are Baum and Kipling.

On the library front similar gestures are noticeable. In Baton Rouge in the winter of 1968-69, a display entitled "Oz—The Wonderful World of L. Frank Baum and His Successors" drew public attention to all Baum's Oz books, "selected titles by the successors," and various items of Baumiana. The sponsoring organization? Louisiana State University Library. Similarly, the Munchkin convention of the IWOC was graciously invited to hold its July, 1971, session in the Community Room of the Free Public Library of Collingswood, New Jersey.

How much of this capitulation is due to the work of the pro-Baum forces and how much would have occurred anyway is of course speculative. But at least one children's book expert sees the renewed interest in Oz as simply a phenomenon of the current Neoromantic Age, the same social force which drew Baum into the orbit of the alternative culture. Fantasy is "in" now and children's book publishers know it, according to Miss Patricia Peart, former assistant editor of Whittlesey

House, the junior books division of McGraw-Hill. Herself author of two books for young people (both non-fantasy),[66] she has also spent eighteen years in library work, and always has a complete set of Oz books on her shelves. Miss Peart says:

> When I was in publishing in the forties, we almost never published fantasy; it just didn't 'go.' Now the current catalogues from children's publishers list [almost] nothing but fantasy or 'problem' books, very few mysteries, very few historical novels such as almost all children love. . . . The Oz books have never lost their appeal for certain children; they circulate steadily from this library, and from others I have worked in. They may be oldfashioned from an adult point of view, and the illustrations are grotesque, but children do not seem to feel either of these things as a handicap.

This judgment of the Oz illustrations as "grotesque" brings up an important digressionary controversy over the comparative merits of the two major illustrators of the Oz books. William Wallace Denslow, who illustrated the original *Wizard*, visualized Dorothy as a pigtailed, ginghamed, sunbonneted little farm girl. In the hands of John Rea Neill, who illustrated the succeeding thirteen books as well as many of the non-Baum Oz books (not to mention some non-Oz Baum books), Dorothy—along with Ozma, Trot, Betsy Bobbin, and the other female Oz characters—became a kind of composite junior Gibson girl, with fluffy hair, an elongated jaw, low-belted frocks, and a disconcerting habit of posing in profile, head thrown back on her shoulders, and more often than not a picture-hat in her slender hand.

In trying to "modernize" Dorothy, however, Neill would seem from this vantage to have dated his own work, while Denslow's retains a kind of whimsical originality which does not pall.

Mrs. Prentice also mentions that the illustrations "date" the books, but defends the textual material for precisely the opposite reason: ". . . there is an almost total absence of any dated views or statements. These books are fantasy and are timeless."[67]

One way or another, then, Baum seems to be receiving a kind of past-due acknowledgement from two influential social strata in America.

★   ★   ★   ★   ★

At a fashionable Santa Barbara residence in 1968, members of the Winkie group of the IWOC met in convention. As is customary, the decorations both inside and out were elaborate, authentic Oz "artifacts." A feature of the program was a costume parade in which eighteen of the conventioneers appeared as familiar Ozites.

When it was over, the story goes, some of the departing guests met "a wandering hippie" outside who had seen and recognized the decorations and costumes and wanted to know how to get to Oz.

"If we knew how to get there, man," he was told, "you wouldn't see us here. . . ."[68]

PART II

Baum's Life and Art: A Contradiction

"Why, you are the only dog I ever heard of who could talk!"

"Except in fairy tales," said Ruffles calmly. "Don't forget the fairy tales."

"I don't forget," replied Tallydab, "but this isn't a fairy tale, Ruffles. It's real life in the kingdom of Noland."

Conversation between
Tallydab and his dog,
Queen Zixi of Ix
(p. 129).

≫ IN *THE LAND OF OZ*, THE SCARECROW SAYS, ". . . I CON-
sider brains far superior to money, in every way. You
may have noticed that if one has money without brains,
he cannot use it to advantage; but if one has brains without money, they will enable him to live comfortably to
the end of his days."[1]

Applying this maxim—reiterated in various forms
elsewhere in Baum's work—to the author's life immediately exposes a curious incompatibility. For if ever a
man was unable to use money to advantage, it was
Baum, and he exhibited his ineptitude again and again.
Nor was he content to "live comfortably to the end of
his days" without it.

Baum's birth only seven years after the California
gold rush, and a youth spent in the "gilded age" of
rapidly expanding national wealth would have exposed
him early to get-rich-quick thinking at its palmiest. Such
a background, combined with the fact that his first professional success was in the theater,[2] evidently had an
effect of concentrating the money-making schemes of
his later life on various kinds of theatrical ventures. And
the older he grew, the more convinced he apparently
became that a fortune was waiting on stage, if he could
just discover the right combination.

Unfortunately for Baum (because of the frustration
which was to follow), the lightning did strike once. The
musical version of *The Wizard* on Broadway and on tour

was a phenomenal success for its time, the turn of the century. But there was no second strike to match it, not in the author's lifetime.

Viewing this lifetime as a struggle to return to the "good days" involves a kind of double exposure when it is additionally recalled that Baum grew up as the indulged son of a wealthy family, and saw his father's fortune lost when he himself was a young man. So the striving after a repetition of his own single-shot stage success (as it must have seemed to him) would surely have been intensified by some impulse, however diffuse or unconscious, to compensate for the family losses.

If Baum can be said to have had an obsession, certainly it revolved around this inability to summon back the opulence and security of the past.

Except, of course, in fancy.

★　　★　　★　　★　　★

There has been a misapprehension among some of the writers about Lyman Frank Baum that he had "an interesting life," even one "as fantastic as his stories." He did not. His childhood was made lonely by a predisposition to ill health which set him apart from his peers, and his adult career was, with a few exceptions, fairly humdrum. True, two of his children's books became immediate "best sellers" at first publication. And a fantastically large correspondence from young readers demanding more and more about Oz was a phenomenon of Baum's later years. But from all indications he seems to have looked upon the former as antecedent events to be read as mere auguries of something more, and upon the latter as a mixed blessing which made him, as a writer, little more than a slave of his admirers.

His birthplace was Chittenango, New York, a small town in the Mohawk Valley, five miles south of Oneida Lake and fifteen miles east of Syracuse, in the same general area as the Oneida Community founded by John Humphrey Noyes in 1838. When Baum was five, his family moved to a fifteen-acre estate, Rose Lawn, just north of Syracuse, in what is now the suburb of Mattydale, and although a second house was maintained in Syracuse proper, it was at Rose Lawn that Baum, seventh of nine children, spent most of his time.

Four of Frank's brothers and sisters did not survive infancy. His own chronic ailment was diagnosed as angina pectoris, a progressive condition which was to circumscribe his activities throughout his life.

Quite understandably, the subject of the ailing heart was never far from the author's thoughts. "Perhaps you have heart disease," says the Tin Woodman to the Lion[3] in an attempt to explain why the Lion's heart beats faster when there is danger. (The Woodman, having at that time no heart himself, knows little about them.) The Woozy says, ". . . my tremendous growl would also frighten you, and if you happen to have heart disease you might expire."[4] One of the twenty-seven officers of the Army of Oz excuses his cowardice with: ". . . I find that I and my brother officers all suffer from heart disease, and the slightest excitement might kill us."[5]

It is the author's own physical condition which gives double meaning to other speeches as well, such as this one of the Woodman: ". . . you must acknowledge that a good heart is a thing that brains can not create, and that money can not buy."[6] And finally, in the last year of life, confined to bed, Baum wrote *The Magic of Oz*, in which Cap'n Bill muses: "There's lots o' things folks don't 'preciate. If somethin' would 'most stop your breath, you'd think breathin' easy was the finest thing in life. When a person's well, he don't realize how jolly it is, but when he gets sick he 'members the time he was well, an' wishes that time would come back. . . ."[7]

This early inclination to illness, combined with the fact that at the time of Baum's childhood the father, Benjamin Ward Baum, was financially sound, even affluent, insured the boy an education without need of attending school. There was one exception, an interlude of less than two academic years beginning in 1868 when Baum at twelve became a cadet at Peekskill Military Academy in his native state. Exactly what happened to the youth at Peekskill has never been made clear, but one can imagine. Why he left is not so much of a mystery. One account[8] says the too-rigorous discipline brought on a "nervous breakdown," and another[9] that the boy had one of his heart attacks.

The Peekskill experience presumably underlies the ridicule of the military in Baum's books. And yet any bias he may have had against military schools themselves was evidently not very wide, since he was to send his own two elder sons to military school,[10] one of whom, Frank Joslyn Baum, later became a career army officer, apparently with his father's considered approval.

After Peekskill, Baum returned to tutorial guidance at home and is supposed to have read variously—though here again there is no data to be counted upon—in compensation for his disinclination to outdoor sports. Dickens has been mentioned as a favorite of Baum's;

Grimm and Andersen he is said to have found repelling because of their "undercurrents of violence and sadness."[11]   He is also supposed to have memorized long passages from Shakespeare and to have been familiar with Thackeray and Charles Reade.[12]   These names hardly make a singular list, but rather one common to many a Victorian reader.   According to one source, Baum was an admirer as well of William Morris,[13] but the Morris work one would expect to become most influential on Baum, *News from Nowhere*, was not published until 1892, so such influence was not early.[14]

References to prevailing literature are not uncommon in the Oz series, and include *Arabian Nights, Aesop's Fables*, and *Pilgrim's Progress* among others. His title *A New Wonderland* (later changed to *The Magical Monarch of Mo*), a non-Oz book, implies familiarity with Lewis Carroll's *Alice*, and there are several sequences in Baum's work in which characters, Alice-like, grow larger or smaller after eating or drinking something magical, including an episode in *The Emerald City* in which Dorothy diminishes in size in order to visit in Bunnyville, where she is received by a rabbit king not unlike the White Rabbit if not the March Hare.

Baum's progenitors had been 1748 settlers in central New York state from the Palatinate; his paternal grandfather, John, was a circuit-riding Methodist lay preacher, and the wealth accumulated by Benjamin came of his being one of the earliest and most enterprising independent developers in the Pennsylvania oil fields.

According to several accounts, the Baum enterprise was eventually reduced to ruin either directly or indirectly by the arrival on the scene of the Standard Oil Company. It is true in any case that the author regarded the company as something of a villain. In *The Sea Fairies*, published in 1911, seven years after Ida Tarbell's *History* would have revived possible old resentments, Trot, the protagonist, insults a would-be friendly octopus in the world of the mermaids by assuming it is "wicked and deceitful." She says, "Up on earth, where I live, they call the Stannerd Oil Company an octopus. . . ." The animal bursts into sobs. "Just because we have several long arms, and take whatever we can reach, they accuse us of being like—like—oh, I cannot say it! It is too shameful—too humiliating!"[15]

But long before the family fortune dwindled, it had financed Baum's experiments in several occupations later to prove helpful when he was faced with having to make his own way against considerable odds.

When he was fifteen, in 1871, he and his younger brother Harry began putting out an amateur newspaper, *The Rose Lawn Home Journal*, using a hand press and a supply of type provided by their father. The project lasted a surprising three years and for two years after that Baum published a "literary" monthly, *The Empire*, with a friend, Thomas G. Alford. Meanwhile, he bred Hamburg chickens at a nearby farm owned by his father, and edited a publication, *The Poultry Record,* for a Syracuse poultry club.

At eighteen, using the name George Brooks, he had also tried to crash into the theater by joining a stock company, a venture which met with no great success. A family anecdote has it that the company manager proved to have more interest in the expensive theatrical wardrobe provided by Baum's father (at the manager's request) than in the young man's acting abilities. In any case, he spent the next two years with Neal, Baum and Company, a dry goods jobbing firm owned by his brother-in-law and father.

At this point he was evidently ready to have another try at the stage. He joined Albert M. Palmer's Union Square Theater in New York as Louis F. Baum. It was at this period too that he is supposed to have spent at least a brief period working for the *New York Tribune*[16] before returning nearer home to Bradford, Pennsylvania, where his father was influential, and where he took a job on the then weekly *Bradford Era* for a year.

Although his biographers do not say so, all these false starts, the theater ventures followed quickly by homecomings to probably less demanding jobs, strongly suggest recurring bouts with angina. But his fascination with the stage was evidently not to be denied, and in 1880 he became manager of a chain of opera houses owned by his father in Olean and Richburg, New York, and in Bradford and Gillmor, Pennsylvania. Shortly after this his father deeded them to him.

From here it must have seemed a natural step to becoming a playwright, and by 1882 he had written three plays: *The Maid of Arran, Matches,* and *The Mackrummins.* The first, a dramatized version of a novel by William Black, *A Princess of Thule*, was modestly successful. It opened at a Baum-owned theater in Gillmor and moved to Manhattan for a season before going on tour.

As the title hints, *The Maid* was an Irish musical comedy with highly sentimental dialogue, plot, and music. Louis F. Baum is listed as author, producer, director, composer, and leading actor. It was the sort of thing then in vogue, but Baum's right to the motif was honestly come by; his mother, Cynthia Stanton, was of Scotch-Irish descent. Later the all-green Emerald City would show continuing loyalty to the author's Celtic heritage.

Baum shrewdly seized the occasion of this ephemeral success to wed (in 1882) Maud Gage of Fayetteville, New York, who is said to have been a Cornell roommate of one of his cousins. The young couple toured with the play until another of the author's bouts with ill health coincided with Maud's first pregnancy, so they returned to a quieter life in Syracuse and Baum again devoted himself to one of his father's businesses, this one a retail outlet for an axle-grease product, Baum's Castorine, while he worked on two more Irish musicals, *Kilmourne*, and *The Queen of Killarney*.

Maud, who emerges in accounts of Baum's later life as a strong-minded realist pitting her foresight and frugality against the whims of her fanciful husband, was the daughter of prominent woman suffragist Mathilda Joslyn Gage, herself author of the book, *Woman, Church and State*, and collaborator with Elizabeth Cady Stanton and Susan B. Anthony on the four-volume *History of Woman Suffrage*,[17] the authoritative contemporaneous document of the movement. Mrs. Gage's name is frequently mentioned in connection with woman suffrage rallies and speeches in the 1870s; one of the high points of her career was the Centennial Exhibition of 1876 in Philadelphia, where she appeared before thousands as a representative of her organization. Her own family had been active Abolitionists and Free Thinkers.

In later years, when Baum's mother-in-law spent some time in the home of her daughter, she is supposed to have had the notion that if some of the stories she overheard Baum telling his children were written down, they would sell. However, given the fact that Baum seemed always to have a fairly sophisticated eye out for the publishable and the potentially popular himself, this story seems to give too much credit to Mrs. Gage, not enough to Baum, except in the matter of gallantry.

Baum seems to have lost his opera house chain in 1884 through a combination of absentee-management and a fire at the Gillmor theater where most of the costumes and scenery were stored. The Castorine outlet also failed, apparently in the general collapse of his father's holdings.

It was about this same time also (1886) that Baum, realizing none of his later Irish melodramas had shown as much promise as the first, began doing other writing. For some of it he drew on his experience with chickens to produce a pamphlet ambitiously called *The Book of Hamburgs: a Brief Treatise Upon the Mating, Rearing and Management of the Different Varieties of Hamburgs.*[18] He seems to have written for various poultry publications as well.

Hamburgs were then the most popular chickens raised for eggs, the predecessors of Leghorns. At least one strain displays a truly odd accomplishment of nature: the fowl are white with large black polkadots. Yet when Baum added a chicken to his collection of Oz characters, he chose not one of the fantastic Hamburgs but a plain "yellow hen." Billina, introduced to the series in *Ozma of Oz*, seems to be either a Buff Orpington or a Buff Plymouth Rock, depending upon what illustration one consults in early editions of *Ozma*.[19] However, since Orpingtons are bred from Hamburgs, it may be presumed Baum had the ochre-colored Orpingtons in mind when he created the talkative Billina, who becomes a tremendous force for good in Oz by laying the eggs which ultimately defeat Roquat of the Rocks (the Nome King), during the group's first encounter with the underworld.

In 1887, his oil fortune wiped out, Benjamin Baum died, and Frank, with his wife and two young sons, struck out for the Middle Border. The Baums apparently selected Aberdeen, South Dakota, because a brother and two sisters of Maud were already there with their families and doing well. Gold had been discovered in the Black Hills of the territory in 1874, and it seems likely that the romantic Frank Baum may have had some idea of making a new fortune in gold country as his father had done in the oil fields a generation earlier. Though photographs taken at the time show Aberdeen as the familiar stereotype of a frontier settlement, with rutted streets and unsubstantial-looking wood-frame facades, the atmosphere there must have held great promise. Until the Baums arrived, anyway. For they had chosen the wrong era. The country was now headed into the slump that would culminate in the Panic of '93.

Baum failed first, in 1889, with a small general store, Baum's Bazaar. The reason given in most accounts is that he was too free with his credit. He failed again two years later after having taken over one of several local newspapers, *The Aberdeen Saturday Pioneer*. While it lasted, though, Baum played his role as frontier journalist with enthusiasm and even flair. His column of entertainment and opinion, "Our Landlady," has been compared with Jerome K. Jerome and Oliver Wendell Holmes (*The Autocrat of the Breakfast Table*). Reading it today can be fairly heavy going, but its burlesques of human frailty and hypocrisy, and the tall tales of fantastic mechanical inventions of the future (Edward Bellamy's *Looking Backward* had been published in 1888) were well received. And the topical nature of some of the columns reflects such conditions as the territory's uneasy Indian situation—the Custer fiasco had occurred only the previous decade—and the oncoming depression, the latter giving rise to a Baum joke about feeding livestock with woodshavings, after the stock had been fitted with green glasses so the shavings would look like grass. In the first Oz book visitors and inhàbitants of the Emerald City wear green glasses to enhance the fraud being perpetrated by the Wizard. Dorothy dons a green dress in the city, but after she leaves discovers that the dress, along with a green bow placed around her dog's neck, has turned white after she removes her glasses. In later books, however, Baum abandons this formula; no one wears glasses, but things are actually green, for under Ozma's rule there is no fraud.

When his Aberdeen paper failed, Baum decided to try Chicago, where he first took a job with the *Chicago Evening Post*, and then became a buyer for the Siegel, Cooper Company crockery department. This in turn led, after a year, to a job as drummer for Pitkin and Brooks, a wholesale china and glassware firm, where he remained for five years.

Robert Stanton Baum, the second of the family's four sons, recalls that his father was also a vendor of fireworks at about this time, and recollects some superb July Fourth celebrations at the Chicago home using his father's road samples. (The gingerbread man in *John Dough* gets to the Isle of Phreex by hanging on too long to an Independence Day rocket.)

But Baum's *bete noir*, the heart condition, again called a halt to what was evidently a lucrative but too-strenuous life, and in 1897 the Baums began living entirely on income derived either from journalism or fiction. Baum began publishing a trade journal, *Show Window*, for retail window trimmers and small merchants interested in exchange of ideas for displaying merchandise. The journal caught on, and in 1900 Baum issued selected articles and illustrations from his magazine as a book: *The Art of Decorating Dry Goods Windows and Interiors.* For a man about to make a mark as a children's writer, such excursions into crockery and shop windows may seem quite far afield. But Baum had for some time now been using all spare intervals for writing, and by this time had in fact already made his debut in juvenile literature.

The Chicago of that time was somewhat of an embryonic center for publishing interests, most of them new in the business, and it was not an impossible achievement for unknown writers to have even marginal work brought out, especially if they were willing to help take some of the financial risk. Baum had maintained contact with the Chicago Press Club, where fledgling publishers occasionally appeared. In 1897 a collection of his children's tales had been published by Way and Williams. Illustrated by Maxfield Parrish—it is also said to have been Parrish's first commercial job—the volume, *Mother Goose in Prose*, was exactly that, a group of prose elaborations of well-known nursery rhymes.

The following year Baum himself, drawing upon his boyhood experience with printing, set up a press in his basement and brought out a collection of verse with the unfelicitous title: *By the Candelabra's Glare.* Some of the entries were illustrated by another press club acquaintance, William Wallace Denslow, who was also to illustrate several more of Baum's books: *Father Goose: His Book*, published in 1899 by George M. Hill; *The Wonderful Wizard of Oz*, 1900, and *Dot and Tot in*

Merryland, 1901, both of these also published by Hill. (Way and Williams had by then dissolved, as Hill also was shortly to do; the mortality as well as the birth rate was high among these new firms.) Denslow also illustrated a Hill edition of *The Songs of Father Goose*, in which the verses from *Father Goose* were set to music by Alberta N. Burton.

Though both *Father Goose* books were financial successes, the first becoming a children's best seller that year, the verse itself depends heavily on the kind of ethnic raillery which is almost (but not entirely) absent from the Oz stories. Chinese, Negro, Irish, Hindu, even Quaker stereotypes are exploited. Typical are:

> Lee-Hi-Lung Whan
> Was a little Chinaman.
> Wooden shoes with pointed toes,
> Almond eyes and tiny nose,
> Pig-tail long and slick and black,
> Clothes the same both front and back,
> Funny little Chinaman,
> Lee-Hi-Lung-Whan.

and

> Patsy Bedad
> Was a bright Irish lad
> Who loved to work hard at his ease;
> 'When I grow up,' said he
> 'I'll a gentleman be,
> For then I shall join the Police.'[20]

The commercial popularity of *Father Goose*, however, brought Baum and Denslow congratulations from such disparate quarters as William Dean Howells and Elbert Hubbard. That the latter should take note of it was hardly surprising, for Denslow spent part of every winter at the Roycroft Colony at East Aurora hand illumining books from the Roycroft Press and drawing cartoons for *The Philistine*. And if Baum's dedication to the styles and values of William Morris had not already put him also into the Hubbard camp, he was certainly there by 1902, when he used proceeds from the lucrative *Father Goose* to purchase and furnish a vacation cottage at Macatawa, Michigan, which he called The Sign of the Goose. At the suggestion of a Chicago heart specialist that he perform some relaxing work, he built furniture and other accessories for the cottage, all in the heavy "overwrought" and selfconsciously quaint fashion of his fellow New Yorker (and for that matter fellow type-setter and book binder), Hubbard. Later, descriptions and illustrations of the court dress in Oz would show a definite Morris-Hubbard influence, if not decadence.

Despite the success of *Father Goose*, for which Denslow and Baum had shared production expenses with the publisher, Hill was willing to publish *The Wizard* only under a similar agreement. However, they did ask Baum to write two other children's books for their list the same year, *The Army Alphabet* and *The Navy Alphabet*, both illustrated by Harry Kennedy, neither really distinguishable from the massive output of other illustrated alphabet books published for beginning readers then and later.

Meanwhile, *A New Wonderland* appeared from New York under the R. H. Russell imprint, illustrated by Frank Verbeck. The fourteen interrelated stories in this collection were later reissued first as *The Surprising Adventures of the Magical Monarch of Mo*, and then simply as *The Magical Monarch of Mo*. The Valley of Mo, one of the fairylands invented by Baum before he wrote *The Wizard*, is a kind of architect's model for the Land of Oz, but with flights which make it less credible than Oz. In Mo:

> The sun shines all the time, and its rays are perfumed. The People who live in the Valley do not sleep, because there is no night. Everything they can possibly need grows on the trees, so they have no use for money at all, and that saves them a deal of worry.
>
> There are no poor people in this quaint Valley. When a person desires a new hat he waits till one is ripe, and then picks it and wears it without asking anybody's permission. . . . There are two rivers in the Land of Mo, one of which flows milk of a very rich quality. Some of the islands in Milk River are made of excellent cheese, and the people are welcome to spade up this cheese whenever they wish to eat it. In the little pools near the bank, where the current does not flow swiftly, delicious cream rises to the top of the milk, and instead of water lilies great strawberry leaves grow upon the surface, and the ripe, red berries lie dipping their noses into the cream. . . . The sand that forms the riverbank is pure white sugar, and all kinds of candies and bonbons grow thick on the low bushes, so that anyone may pluck them easily . . . it rains in Mo as it

does everywhere else, only it rains lemonade;
and the lightning in the sky resembles the
most beautiful fireworks, and the thunder is
usually a chorus from the opera of "Tann-
hauser."

No one ever dies in this Valley, and the people
are always young and beautiful.[21]

Other Baum books of this period—the first two
years of the new century were the author's most prolific
as far as sheer numbers of things published—were *American Fairy Tales*,· published by Hill and illustrated by
Ike Morgan et al., and *The Master Key*, an early
excursion into the socalled "science fiction" genre published in Indianapolis by Bowen-Merrill and illustrated
by Fanny Cory, both of these in 1901. *The Life and
Adventures of Santa Claus*, published by Bowen-Merrill
and illustrated by Mary Cowles Clark, and *The Enchanted Island of Yew*, from Bobbs-Merrill, illustrated
by Fanny Cory, followed in 1902 and 1903 respectively.

None of these books of course approached *The
Wizard* as an artistic or financial success, and it was the
Wizard alone who really launched the careers of both
Denslow and Baum. Robert Stanton Baum recalls both
the author and the illustrator shortly after the book's
success had become a fact:

Father had now become a budding author
and had written *Mother Goose in Prose*, the
Army and Navy Alphabets, *The Wizard of Oz*,
and was now working on the musical extravaganza which was later destined to bring him a
lot of fame and fortune. Paul Tejens [sic]
was writing the music and many evenings he

would come over to the house to work with
father.   Denslow, who drew the original pictures for *The Wizard of Oz*, was also a frequent
visitor.   I can remember the three of them
cutting up like a bunch of school boys.
Tejens would pound out a piece on the piano
and father would sing the words or perhaps do
a tap or eccentric dance, accompanied by the
ferocious looking Denslow, who was a thick
set man with a heavy 'walrus' mustache and
looked like a brigand.   It was better than a
vaudeville show to us boys. . . .[22]

This was it, then: the brink of the single season of
real theatrical success. The play was to run for nine
years, 1902 to 1911, opening in Chicago and moving to
New York in 1903. By the time the script reached the
stage, however, it had been so revised by producer-
director Julian Mitchell that it bore practically no
resemblance to Baum's book. Dorothy had become a
nubile milkmaid with a pet cow, Imogene; a Lady
Lunatic had been added to the cast, along with a poet
prince with whom Dorothy falls in love. Other ingredients included chorus girls, a Maypole dance, an Irish jig,
Highland fling, cake walk, and an Irish comic cast as
the Wizard. Something for everybody. The Scarecrow
and Woodman were still there, though, and the roles
brought resounding fame to comedians Fred Stone and
Dave Montgomery.
    At first Baum is said to have greeted the changes
with dismay. Later, when success for the musical was
assured, he wrote a letter to the *Chicago Tribune* which
—if it is sincere or not, as has been suggested, a publicity
ploy—is surely some kind of precedent in author capitu-

lation to popular taste:

> . . . I confess, after two years of success for the extravaganza, that I now regard Mr. Mitchell's views in a different light. The people will have what pleases them, and not what the author happens to favor, and I believe that one of the reasons why Julian Mitchell is recognized as a great producer is that he faithfully tries to serve the great mass of playgoers—and usually succeeds.
>
> My chief business is, of course, the writing of fairy tales, but should I ever attempt another extravaganza, or dramatize another of my books, I mean to profit by the lesson Mr. Mitchell has taught me, and sacrifice personal preference to the demands of those I shall expect to purchase admission tickets. . . .[23]

Now the push was on in earnest. The conditional ". . . should I ever attempt . . ." was pure rhetoric, for by this time (1904) Baum had already made the attempt, more than once.

Daniel P. Mannix[24] has theorized that it was this same single-minded pursuit of a second dramatic success of the same magnitude as the first that prompted the curious subject matter and handling of the second Oz book, *The Marvelous Land of Oz*, published in 1904. The very fact that the book was originally to be called *The Further Adventures of the Scarecrow and the Tin Woodman* would seem to indicate that Baum or his publishers wanted to borrow on the fame of Stone and Montgomery on Broadway, if not create new roles for the comedians with a second play.

A further application of this argument would also clear up a problem that has mildly perplexed readers for years: how did Baum happen to select a burlesque on the suffragist movement as a suitable topic for a children's book? From a producer's-eye-view, however, what better spectacle for a musical farce than an all-girl army? In *The Land of Oz* there is also a field of sunflowers with girls' faces, a device more appropriate to the world of Florenz Ziegfeld than that of Baum. *Land* is also the first Oz book to depend heavily on puns for humor. Part of Mitchell's formula for success had been the addition of numerous puns to the script of *The Wizard.*

While punning can scarcely be listed as a convention of children's literature, the author lays careful groundwork in *Land* when the pompous Woggle-Bug explains:

'A joke derived from a play upon words is considered among educated people to be eminently proper. . . . It means . . . that our language contains many words having a double meaning; and that to pronounce a joke that allows both meanings of a certain word, proves the joker is a person of culture and refinement, who has, moreover, a thorough command of the language. . . . I say that puns display genius. For instance, were I to ride upon this Saw-Horse, he would [become] an equipage. For he would then be a horse-and-buggy.'[25]

And yet for the children this kind of foolery doesn't quite come off sometimes. It might be argued that a pun comprehensible to young readers is provided when the Woggle-Bug warns Jack Pumpkinhead that if he drops his head, it would ". . . no longer be a pumpkin, for it would become a squash." But it is something else again when, after General Jinjur has threatened to make tarts of the pumpkinhead, the Woodman says: "Don't worry. It cannot matter greatly. If you stay shut up here you will spoil in time, anyway. A good tart is far more admirable than a decayed intellect."

Even the sex change in *Land* by which the male hero turns into a female princess may have its roots in Baum's dramatic aspirations. Mannix reminds us that it is a tradition of pantomime that boys' roles were sometimes played by girls who appeared in elaborate feminine dress in the finale.

In any case, Baum wasted no time. Unaided, he turned *Land* into an "extravaganza" called *The Woggle-Bug*, which opened in Chicago in 1905, and although the hardy *Wizard* musical kept on running, the second show closed in three weeks. Evidently the puns, the girl-flowers, and the female army, though highly derivative of Mitchell, were not the right combination after all.

The second book about Oz sold well as children's literature, however, as did Baum's other books of this time, and on the strength of this and the show still playing on the road, Baum and his wife went abroad in 1906. The "grand tour" included France, Switzerland, Egypt, Greece, Italy, and North Africa. Baum fell all too easily into the role of philistine American tourist. He is quoted as remarking that the sight of the Statue of Liberty, on their return, was the best of the trip.[26]

Small wonder that it must have seemed to Baum that these crowded years were the apogee of his career, that his later work was all downhill by comparison.

And yet such a judgment rests with far more accuracy upon his two principal business associates of these times, Denslow and Paul Tietjens. Denslow, a newspaper artist and cartoonist before he began illustrating books for children in collaboration with Baum, fell out with the writer shortly after publication of *The Wizard* and never illustrated another Baum book. Apparently the quarrel centered around whether it was the author or the artist who was ultimately to be credited with the success of their work, and more specifically on how much Denslow was to receive from the show. (He had designed some costumes and sets, but his work was evidently passed over in favor of a designer from Mitchell's circle.)

Although Denslow subsequently joined the *New York Herald* staff and also illustrated children's books by other writers, he never "made it back." That he himself saw his plight as a case of literally being driven out of Oz is obvious from the fact that he later wrote and illustrated a book called *The Scarecrow and the Tin Man*, with illustrations almost identical to those he had done for Baum, but no mention of Oz. According to several accounts, Denslow died penniless in Buffalo in 1915.

Nor was Tietjens the composer to achieve any other professional success remotely comparable to the musical made of *The Wizard*, although he too strove hard for the rest of his life after another brass ring. Several of these tries were again in collaboration with Baum, and it was of the time when the two were at work together at the Baum resort cottage in Macatawa that Eunice Tietjens, then Paul's wife, speaks when she describes Baum as "tall and rangy, with an imagination and a vitality which constantly ran away with him. . . .

Constantly exercising his imagination as he did, he had come to the place where he could honestly not tell the difference between what he had done and what he imagined. Everything he said had to be taken with at least half a pound of salt."[27]

Following her divorce from the composer several years after this, the poet Eunice Tietjens became far better known than her husband. Involved with the "imagist" movement, she was assistant editor to Harriet Monroe on *Poetry* magazine. Meanwhile, however, Paul Tietjens disappeared from the arts-and-letters circle of which Chicago had become the hub, and on the periphery of which Baum rotated, awaiting another chance.

The cursory physical description of Baum given by the composer's wife coincides with others of him, and with photographs. Baum was a large man, over six feet tall and substantially built for all his delicate health. And without doubt he would be considered handsome by the standards of any age, with dark, abundant hair, eyes that can only be called "dreamy," and an outgoing, friendly manner. He also had a tendency to dandyism, and after prosperity touched him affected white vests in the manner of William McKinley, along with suits of obviously expensive cut and now and then an obvious jeweled tie-tack, or lapel flower. In the Edwardian Age, he must have been a true conformist.

After the *Woggle-Bug* musical proved a flop, Baum tried (in 1908-9) a new medium which he called "Fairylogue and Radio Plays," and into which he incautiously poured more of his own capital than he had risked on any of his prior plans. The venture, carried out as a business arrangement with the Selig Polyscope Company, which handled the technical side, had nothing to do with radio, an invention then in infancy, but the word was

more or less "in the air" at the time. Exactly what it
meant to Baum in this connection is not clear, but the
project involved a series of hand-tinted moving films—
cinema was then new—showing scenes from Baum's
books, while he stood by as narrator. The production,
which was already proving far too expensive for its
returns before it left Chicago theaters, did move to
New York City, but was given up as a bad job shortly
thereafter.

  This financial disaster was very soon followed by
another. Instead of an Oz book in 1911, Baum had
turned out *The Sea Fairies*, an underwater adventure
reminiscent of E. Nesbit's *Wet Magic*. It sold only
12,401 copies as opposed to *The Emerald City*'s 20,000
the previous year.[28]   Baum declared personal bankruptcy, listing his debts at $12,600 and his assets as
"two suits of clothes and a typewriter."[29]   Then, on
the advice of his publishers, he retreated in haste once
more to Oz, where the steady money was. Although
one more non-Oz fantasy, *Sky Island*, a companion
work to *The Sea Fairies*, was already in the mill and
came off press in 1912, Baum had *The Patchwork Girl
of Oz* ready for publication in 1913.

  And once again he had climbed out of his financial
difficulties in order that he could plunge immediately
back in. This time he wrote another "extravaganza,"
The Tik-Tok Man of Oz, and it is a testimony to the
seriousness with which he still took the Julian Mitchell
formula that the production had a full chorus of roses
with girls' faces. Also, like the stage version of the
Wizard, *Tik-Tok* began with a roaring storm. Actress
Charlotte Greenwood appeared as Queen Ann Soforth,
another female commandant, her army not of girls this
time but of comic characters. The musical opened in

Los Angeles, where Baum was then living, in 1913, and then went on tour. A new team of comedians, James Morton as Tik-Tok, the machine man, and Frank Moore as the Shaggy Man, attempted to duplicate the popularity of Montgomery and Stone, and though *Tik-Tok* did far better than *The Woggle-Bug* (or for that matter the "radio" venture), it was no *Wizard*.

However, Baum reused the dramatized material in the children's book of the same title, which came out in 1914 dedicated to Louis F. Gottschalk, who had done the musical score for the play. The book was hailed with enthusiasm by Baum's loyal child readership.

Now might have been a time for Baum to quit while he was ahead, or at least running even. Instead the indefatigable author that same year formed the Oz Film Manufacturing Company, this time risking the capital of several partners, and began shooting film versions of his books. Perhaps *this* was the way to get rich quick.

Selig Pictures (which had no known connection with Baum in a business way, but was apparently a successor to the ill-fated Selig Polyscope which still owned the tinted lantern slides used in the Radio Plays) had in 1910 already produced *The Wizard* without notable success. (And after Baum's death, Chadwick Pictures was to make still another silent version of the story with Larry Semon as the Scarecrow and Oliver Hardy as the Woodman.)

The Oz Company, predictably, was in financial difficulty almost from the beginning, although five films were finished: *The Patchwork Girl, His Majesty the Scarecrow of Oz* (later retitled *The New Wizard of Oz*), *The Magic Cloak* (based on *Queen Zixi of Ix*, which is subtitled *The Magic Cloak*), *The Last Egyptian* (based on Baum's anonymous adult novel of that title), and something by Baum called *The Gray Nun of Belgium*. When it became obvious that none of these ventures would recoup the considerable expenditures of the firm, the Oz Company closed down and its studios were offered for lease.

While, as we have seen, most of Baum's bids for crash success were directed in one way or another toward the dramatic arts, not all fit the category. Since 1905 the Baums had been spending the winter months in Coronado, California, and that year, according to biographical accounts, Baum bought Pedloe Island, some eighty miles off the San Diego shore, apparently with plans to turn it into a kind of Baumian Disneyland (if this is not a contradiction in terms), or at least an amusement park in the shape of a miniature Land of Oz.

The only trouble with this story is that no Pedloe Island in this location (or in fact any other location on the Pacific offshore) shows on any map of the area or in any standard reference, including the ultra-thorough Coast and Geodetic Survey published by the U. S. Department of Commerce. Nor is there any other piece of land of this description in the general area. But the tendency of magic islands and fairylands like Oz to disappear without warning is a topic to be discussed in the following section. Perhaps this happened to Pedloe.

Whatever the project was, Baum's investment, along with the plan, seems to have been lost during one of the many crises, and one wonders if it were not for the best. Oz was already coming in for plenty of exploitation at the hands of Baum's permanent publisher, Reilly and Britton (Reilly and Lee after 1918), who were soon cranking out Oz picture books, Oz coloring books, an edition to be given away as a prize with breakfast cereal, and other specialties by the hundred gross, and sponsoring a widespread newspaper competition in connection with Oz comics.

Inevitably, in dealing with the few ups and many downs of Baum's financial adventures, one sees a parallel case in the story of Baum's contemporary Samuel Clemens. Both began with some knowledge of typography and became journalists, but the more striking similarity is the fact that both, after a substantial literary success, apparently became convinced that the "real" money lay elsewhere; then, after single or multiple disastrous disillusionments on this score, they retreated to writing or related activity to make up their losses. With his royalties from *Innocents Abroad*, Clemens made his abortive excursion into publishing, eventually fastening all his hopes upon the Paige typesetting machine. This latter monument to the ingenuity of its inventor, which functioned with movable type automatically positioned, was ultimately superseded by the Merganthaler Linotype, which operated on the far more efficient principle of movable matrices into which the lead is poured to produce a solid type line. But not before the Paige machine had literally cleaned Clemens out financially. Like Baum, he declared bankruptcy, but made a strenuous world lecture tour in order, later, to repay his creditors in full.

And yet these two cases are hardly isolated instances. As we have already noted, the rags-to-riches formula and the legends of sudden, easy wealth were simply part of the atmosphere of the last quarter of the nineteenth century and at least the first decade of the twentieth, and anyone who breathed that atmosphere was quite likely to become infected. It is true, however, that there is something central to the occupation of writing which would make writers perhaps more vulnerable to schemes of rapid wealth than others, especially those writers who have achieved one signal success. For there is nothing like success to make a writer lose confidence; he wonders how he did it and becomes convinced he can never do it again. Hence he must cast about for some other way to make money while he still has the wherewithal to manage it. Unlike Clemens, son of a country barrister, Baum had already experienced the riches-to-rags descent, which may very well make his case the more poignant after all.

Beginning in 1909, the Baums had made their permanent home in Los Angeles, where the author became as much of an outdoorsman as his health would permit, engaged in gardening, boating, archery, and golf. In 1910 a japonesque bungalow-mansion in the Richardson style was built for them on what is now Cherokee Avenue near Sunset Boulevard in Hollywood, and Baum's bent for drama was at least partly channeled into entertainment for the Uplifters, a social group he helped found, and which included most of the leading lights of the new film industry.

To say that Baum's preoccupation with dramatic success and its resultant financial disturbances affected his writing may well amount to an understatement of the obvious. How much of the profusion of pseudonymous material Baum would have hacked out, however, if he had not kept himself more or less constantly in debt, is less certain. It is true that during these hectic years he became one of those rarities dear to the hearts of commercial publishers, the all-purpose series writer.

As "Captain Hugh Fitzgerald" he wrote two books for boys about the adventures of a hero called Sam Steele; these, published in 1906-7, were reissued in 1908-11, along with four additional titles, as The Boy

Fortune Hunters series by "Floyd Akers." (One Baum expert has suggested this pseudonym derives from "F. Aker," or "faker.")

A set of six duodecimo volumes for very young children, with animal titles and subjects along lines of the Beatrix Potter books, came out in 1906 by "Laura Bancroft" and were later reissued as a single volume. But the most long-lived and popular series stories, next to Oz, were the Aunt Jane's Nieces books which emerged almost annually from 1906 to 1915 by "Edith Van Dyne." "She" also began another series, Mary Louise, in 1916 which ran to five volumes, but the Nieces remained the favorites and the series, again like Oz, was carried on by other writers after Baum's death. Still another book for adolescent girls, *Annabel*, had appeared in 1906 by "Suzanne Metcalf."

Then there are Baum's three adult novels, none of these written under his own name either: *The Fate of a Crown*, 1905, a romance set in Brazil (where Baum had never been), and *Daughters of Destiny*, 1906, both of these by "Schuyler Staunton." *The Last Egyptian*, a novel of intrigue set in contemporary Egypt, came out anonymously in 1908.

It would be convenient, from the standpoint of presenting Baum as a homogeneous person whose writing showed consistency of whatever kind, to be able to make some generalization about these additional Baum writings. This is not, however, a possibility except to say that of the whole Baum oeuvre, nothing really approaches in excellence the early better known fairy tales, a list which includes *John Dough*, *Queen Zixi*, and the first three or four (or perhaps five) Oz books.

The relative popularity of Aunt Jane's Nieces apparently stemmed from the acceptability of the young-woman-against-the-world story to readers of the time. At least there were a great many similar series then and later (the Nancy Drew series goes on even today), and Baum's seems in no way distinguished from others of the type, unless one counts the fact that his heroine was collective: the three nieces of John Merrick, a puckish millionaire. Merrick himself is a depressing stereotype, something of a cross between Dickens' Brothers Cheeryble in *Nicholas Nickleby* and Daddy Warbucks. Dogooder Merrick goes about spreading cheer, touting the virtues of industry and frugality, and righting wrongs with his money, while the nieces, also radiating happiness and impeccable honesty, plunge into all sorts of business and social adventures where their goodness is bound to meet up with evil forces. Virtue, however, is never enough to bring off a solution, so Baum provides a *deus ex machina* in the form of an also-stereotyped private detective, Quintus Fogerty, retained, of course, by Uncle John for the very purpose of extricating the girls when necessary.

Lack of distinction also marks Baum's writing for younger children, with a possible exception in the story "A Kidnapped Santa Claus," which appeared in *The Delineator* of December, 1904, and has been recently republished as a children's book.[30] Clearly a morality tale, in which the Daemons of Selfishness, Envy, Hatred, and Malice, jealous of Santa Claus, tie him up and hide him on Christmas Eve, the story is at the same time a fast-moving, satisfying adventure. Santa's staff of ryls, knooks, pixies, and fairies saves the day, or rather the night, by delivering the presents, and the prisoner is released by the Daemon of Repentance, a brother of the villains and one of their own kind because, as Repentance himself says: "Of course it is too late to remedy the evil that has been done; but repentance, you know, can come only after an evil thought or deed, for in the beginning there is nothing to repent of." To which Santa replies: "So I understand. . . . Those who avoid evil need never visit your cave."

The Baum short stories written for adult and youth audiences and appearing in various magazines of the time are as a rule, however, little better than the adult novels. Typical are "The Tramp and the Baby," which appeared in *The Ladies' World* of October, 1911, and "Aunt Huldah's Good Time," from *The Youth's Companion* of October 26, 1899, a story which later appeared in *St. Nicholas* magazine (December, 1912) under the title "Aunt Phroney's Boy." The chief characteristic of both these stories is a suppurating sentimentality scarcely matched anywhere outside the novels of Gene Stratton Porter.

Quite another kind of flaw marks "The Suicide of Kiaros," first published in *The White Elephant* of September, 1897, and reprinted in *Ellery Queen's Mystery Magazine* in November, 1954. Here too stereotypes abound: the embezzling cashier betrothed to the boss's daughter; the daughter, "a beautiful girl and an acknowledged leader in society"; the exotic foreign money-lender, who in this case is for some reason a Greek instead of a Jew. The opening paragraph might be a parody on opening paragraphs for such stories:

> Mr. Felix Marston, cashier for the great mercantile firm of Van Alsteyne & Traynor, sat in his little private office with a balance sheet before him and a frown upon his handsome face. At times he nervously ran his slim fingers through the mass of dark hair that clus-

tered over his forehead, and the growing
expression of annoyance upon his features
fully revealed his disquietude.[31]

Moreover, for reasons never explained, Kiaros the
money-lender speaks with inverted syntax. ("A satisfactory debter you have ever proved," said he, "and to
pay me with promptness never failed. . . . To my congratulations you are surely entitled . . . to lose Mr. Van
Alsteyne's confidence would leave me to collect the sum
wholly unable.") If such speech is meant to simulate
accented English, the effect is surely more Teutonic
than Greek.

But it is not the high rate of cliché or even the
untrue dialect which really mars the tale. The cashier
who has gambled away the firm's funds applies to the
money-lender and is refused; in a peculiarly depressing
scene he kills Kiaros with a paper knife, takes what he
wants from the Greek's safe, and makes the murder into
a suicide by locking the door from the outside but
returning the key to the desk inside the room through
a panel in the door with a string running to the desk.
The string is then removed. It is apparently this trick
alone which is the raison d'etre for the story, since
nothing else happens except that the cashier's accounts
are audited and pronounced sound, he marries the boss's
daughter and becomes a member of the firm and a
respectable citizen, and the police never suspect the
suicide isn't a suicide. But the trick which has made
possible the "perfect crime" doesn't seem enough to
make up for the lack of resolution, nor does Baum's
final paragraph in which we discover the cashier has
confessed to the narrator of the story, identified only as
"me." The piece does provide some moments of un-

conscious humor, however, as for instance in the long rumination of the cashier as he bends over the body of his victim:

> 'He was a very good fellow, old Kiaros,' he murmured. 'I am sorry I had to kill him. But this is no time for regrets; I must try to cover all traces of my crime. The reason most murderers are discovered is because they become terrified, are anxious to get away, and so leave clues behind them. I have plenty of time. Probably no one knows of my visit here tonight, and as the old man lives alone, no one is likely to come here before morning.'[32]

Such a detailed treatment of one of Baum's lesser known stories will at least serve to point up still another major contradiction in Baum, this one well nigh inexplicable. How is it possible that the same man who performed so splendidly in *The Wizard* could have written so badly elsewhere? Such disparities often show up in material taken from different periods of a writer's career, but these two were written at approximately the same time.

A brief glimpse into how Baum viewed himself as a writer may be provided in an inscription to his sister on a copy of *Mother Goose in Prose*.

> *My dear Mary: When I was young I longed to write a great novel that should win me fame. Now that I am getting old my first book is written to amuse children. For, aside from my evident inability to do anything 'great,' I have learned to regard fame as a will-o-the-*

wisp which, when caught, is not worth the possession; but to please a child is a sweet and lovely thing that warms one's heart and brings its own reward. . . .[33]

Perhaps this compromise with "fame" was genuine, at least for the moment of the writing of the inscription; one suspects, however, that the words reflect a bit of the self-delusion which emerges as characteristic of Baum. It would be even more satisfactory to be able to regard his apparent acceptance here of the role of children's writer as sincere. Yet he did not, after this, exactly "settle down" to children's writing any more than he abandoned the familiar pattern of "go for broke" attempts to return to better times (and more fame?). There is no real indication anywhere that he ever regarded even his Oz material as anything but a means to some other end.

And if recurring heart attacks, complicated by painful seizures of tic douloureux and complications arising from a gallbladder operation, had not kept him bedridden for the last eighteen months of his life, he could surely be imagined carrying the money-making schemes to ever more delirious heights.

"We long for what we cannot have," muses Queen Zixi of Ix, "yet desire it not so much because it would benefit us, as because it is beyond our reach."

★   ★   ★   ★   ★

Many readers feel that if any of Baum's work can be called autobiographical, it is *Dot and Tot of Merry-*

land, a fairy tale in which, as in the Oz series, children from the United States travel to the fairy country and return. Dot and Tot are, respectively, the daughter of a banker and the son of a gardener. They live on an estate called Roselawn, Baum's nostalgic descriptions of which —if not the name itself—identify it as his boyhood home. Also, his own father was, among other things, a "banker," one of the founders and a member of the board of a Syracuse bank.

There is far more to be learned about the "real" Frank Baum, however, scattered throughout his other writings, particularly the Oz series. For instance, we have the up-and-down spirit of the profligate born to wealth but doomed to privation in Baum's portrayal of Dorothy's Uncle Henry. This uncle, however, is Baum's true mirror image, properly reversed, for he is born to privation. Pictured in the first book as an impecunious Kansas farmer, living in a one-room cabin, scraping a bare subsistence from the dusty gray plain, he unaccountably appears two books later (*Ozma of Oz*) voyaging to Australia for his health. Illustrator John R. Neill complies with the new image by providing a picture of Uncle Henry in spats, embroidered vest, string tie, boiled shirt, and velvet-collared smoking jacket, seated in a wing-chair in Sydney, thoughtfully attending a briar pipe. No hint of how this remarkable switch in fortunes came about is offered, nor why Henry was so unfeeling as to have left Aunt Em "at home to watch after the hired men and to take care of the farm. . . ."

Sure enough, though, his luck doesn't last. We meet him three books farther along (*The Emerald City*) back in straw hat and bib overalls, on the brink of a mortgage foreclosure on the farm. This time, though, there is a brief history of his financial misadventures:

Dorothy Gale lived on a farm in Kansas, with her Aunt Em and her Uncle Henry. It was not a big farm, nor a very good one, because sometimes the rain did not come when the crops needed it, and then everything withered and dried up. Once a cyclone had carried away Uncle Henry's house, so that he was obliged to build another; and as he was a poor man he had to mortgage his farm to get the money to pay for the new house. Then his health became bad and he was too feeble to work. The doctor ordered him to take a sea voyage and he went to Australia and took Dorothy with him. That cost a lot of money too.

Uncle Henry grew poorer every year, and the crops raised on the farm only brought food for the family. Therefore the mortgage could not be paid. At last the banker who had loaned him the money said that if he did not pay on a certain day, his farm would be taken away from him.[34]

We know that Baum's own father, toward the end of his life, went to Germany for medical treatment after an accident with a shying horse. But then Baum's father, as we have seen, was not a Kansas dirt farmer. Uncle Henry's problems are ended, of course, when he and Aunt Em retire in Oz.

Another aspect of Baum's life difficult to pin down from factual accounts but presented with perspicuity in his fiction has to do with his religious convictions.

The household in which he grew up was apparently Methodist, with family Bible reading sessions and prohibitions against Sunday diversion. Except for membership in an Episcopal church in Aberdeen, he appears to have had no affiliation with churches as an adult, although for a time he is supposed to have been attracted to Theosophy.[35]   Maud's own background may have prompted the decision to send Baum's sons to an Ethical Culture Sunday school when they lived in Chicago, but evidently neither parent became involved with this movement.

There is no mention of church-going in Oz, and the only reference to a church building is in *The Wizard*, when the group accidentally breaks a china cow and a church in passing through the Dainty China Country. Dorothy expresses relief that they've done "no worse damage."

Otherwise, so far as Oz is concerned, the closest Baum comes to admitting that formal religion exists— and it is not very close—is in a description of Utensia (*The Emerald City*), a country where King Cleaver rules over an assortment of sentient kitchen implements, among which is a High Priest Colender [sic]. "He's the high priest because he is the holiest thing we have in the kingdom."

Yet for all of this, the Land of Oz is rich in Judeo-Christian paraphernalia. One has only to look at Baum's imaginary world in the light of mythic Christianity to note the striking similarity between the Emerald City and traditional glimpses of the City of God. The former is

> . . . built all of beautiful marbles in which are set a profusion of emeralds, every one exquisitely cut and of very great size. There are other jewels used in the decorations inside the houses and palaces, such as rubies, dia-

monds, sapphires, amethysts and turquoises.
But in the streets and upon the outside of the
buildings only emeralds appear. . . .[36]

And when Dorothy and her party visit the Valley
of Voe (*Dorothy and the Wizard*), they learn that they
must not eat the Dama fruit, which is virtually irresist-
ible but forbidden if one wants to remain visible. It
requires all Dorothy's fortitude to overcome the temp-
tation.

In the same book the friends save themselves from
the invisible bears ("an unseen danger is always hardest
to face") by rubbing the soles of their shoes and the
tires of their buggy with a magic plant which enables
them to walk, Christ-like (or Buddha-like, if one pre-
fers), onto a stream and proceed down it where the
bears cannot follow.

It is not in Oz, however, but in the Noland presented in *Queen Zixi of Ix* that Baum reaches the apogee
of this flight. Bud, poverty-stricken and hungry, on his
journey to the capital city, Nole, is denied room at an
inn but allowed to sleep in its stable. In the morning he
rides through the city gates mounted on a donkey and,
because he is the forty-seventh person to pass through
(Baum would have been forty-seven the year this book
was written), is received with jubilation and crowned
king.

Enthroned, King Bud provides still another whimsical burlesque of biblical lore when he tries to dispense
justice in the matter of two women disputing ownership
of a cow. He shrewdly awards the animal to the woman
for whom the cow stands to be milked. The victorious
woman then admits she stole the cow from the other
woman, and the animal has stood still only because she,

the thief, is more adept as a milkmaid.

The Enchanted Island of Yew also contains a direct allusion to Christian theology: "Mortals can't become fairies, you know—although I believe there was once a mortal who was made immortal."[37]

On another level, Baum's work is liberally inset with explicit moral injunctions, most of them little more than wall-motto aphorisms in the manner of Samuel Smiles. "Advice doesn't cost anything—unless you follow it . . ," counsels the wise donkey in *The Patchwork Girl*. And Button-Bright (in *The Lost Princess*) observes: "Always, when there's trouble, there's a way out of it, if you can find it." Woot the Wanderer (*The Tin Woodman*) remarks in almost the same style: "Fear does not make one a coward . . . but I believe it is more easy to avoid danger than to overcome it. The safest way is the best way, even for one who is brave and determined."

It is the implicit message, however, which speaks loudest in Baum, and if a generality can be made, it is a sense of moral relativism—undoubtedly the author's own—which emerges. To mean well, to do the best one can, to make sure the end justifies the means—these are the impulses required of Baum heroes and heroines, along with the ability to assume a stoic posture in the face of all danger or reversal of fortune.

The Shaggy Man, it turns out, has stolen the Love Magnet, but since the victim of the theft was someone who definitely did not need such an amulet—a young girl with too many suitors—no word of reproach is ever spoken. And it is Dorothy's outright theft of the Nome King's magic belt which is a direct cause of the invasion of the Land of Oz (in *The Emerald City*), which in turn nearly results in destruction of the fairyland. But pre-

sumably in the hands of Dorothy and Ozma the belt will
be used only for good purposes, while the Nome King
works evil with it, thus Dorothy steals with impunity.
An analogous situation serves as the rationale for *John
Dough*, since the Arab is the rightful owner of the Elixir
of Life and Mme. Leontyne deprives him of that ownership.   She does so, furthermore, without the Arab's
having done anything to her but bestow upon her an
invaluable cure for her rheumatism.   The point to keep
in mind, however, is that Mme. Leontyne's clear action
of returning evil for good was in the nature of an honest
mistake; she was well intentioned, thus the Arab, trying
to recover his stolen property, becomes the villain.

Early evidence that to mean well is to be beyond
responsibility occurs in *The Wizard*. The death of the
first wicked witch is plainly an accident; Dorothy's
house falls on her. But responsibility for the death of
the second is not so clearcut. Dorothy deliberately sets
out on an errand of destruction when she searches out
the witch, reluctantly or not, and the little girl single-
handedly causes the witch's demise (or disintegration).
Yet because Dorothy does not know water is harmful to
the witch, and does not *mean* to kill, there is no culpa-
bility.

It is intention that makes the difference again in a
reversal of the idea (*Dorothy and the Wizard*) after
Eureka's trial, when the kitten is still shunned by the
Ozites "in spite of the fact she had not eaten the piglet.
For the folks of Oz knew the kitten had tried to commit
the crime and that only an accident had prevented her
from doing so; therefore even the Hungry Tiger preferred
not to associate with her."

Even in minor matters it is intentions that count.
In *Ozma*, for instance, Dorothy defends Billina, who has

frightened the Nome King, by admitting: "She may not always be 'zactly polite; but she *means* well, I'm sure."

If good is not always absolute in Oz, neither is evil. The Nome King himself, arch enemy of Oz, is not really considered such a bad sort in the first encounters of the protagonal group with him. "The Nome King is honest and good natured," says Tik-Tok (*Ozma*). "You can trust him to do what is right." Similarly (in *The Sea Fairies*), Sacho reflects: "There is no one in all the world so bad that there is nothing good about him." Elsewhere, evil is transformed to good by love, or is sometimes vanquished by ignoring it. The impassable barrier, which recurs frequently in Baum, is this latter kind of evil. If one pays it no heed, or simply shuts his eyes, it will go away. Typical of these episodes is one in *The Patchwork Girl*; Scraps and her party find their way barred by a high iron wall, but the Shaggy Man orders them to close their eyes and follow him. They do, and "to their astonishment found the wall and the gateway far behind them. . . ." Shaggy explains: "That wall . . . is what is called an optical illusion. It is quite real while you have your eyes open, but if you are not looking at it the barrier doesn't exist at all. It's the same way with many other evils in life; they seem to exist, and yet it's all seeming and not true."[38] And in *The Tin Woodman* the Scarecrow pontificates: "If you think of some dreadful thing, it's liable to happen . . . but if you don't think of it, and no one else thinks of it, it just can't happen."[39]

That evil may be illusory serves also as the basic assumption behind Baum's many exposures of the dreadful and the much-feared as fraud. In addition to the primary instance of the Wizard himself, there are (*Ozma of Oz*) the Wheelers, frightful because of the noises they make, but they are easily defeated by Tik-Tok, who merely picks the leader up and shakes him. The leader bursts immediately into tears.

> 'Now I and my people are ruined forever!' he sobbed; 'for you have discovered our secret. Being so helpless, our only hope is to make people afraid of us, by pretending we are very fierce and terrible, and writing in the sand warnings to Beware the Wheelers. Until now we have frightened everyone, but since you have discovered our weakness our enemies will fall upon us and make us very miserable and unhappy.'[40]

But Dorothy promises the secret will be kept on condition the Wheelers not "try to frighten children any more, if they come near to you." And there is King Terribus (*Yew*), so frightful he does not allow himself to be seen. Yet Prince Marvel avoids death by changing the king's ugly appearance, which in turn improves his disposition, so he is not terrible after all.

As a side commentary here, Terribus, like the Shaggy Man's brother, the Ugly One (*Tik-Tok*), represents another recurring Baum motif in which a repulsive character hides himself from others because of physical deformity. Interestingly, for an author who elsewhere touts the virtues of individuality and full acceptance by the group no matter what singularity is presented, the deformed characters are never ultimately tolerated as they are, "warts and all." Rather their eventual acceptance depends inevitably and wholly upon a magical transformation which renders them attractive, or at least more like other people.

It is perhaps to be expected that the same brand of Emersonian optimism which insists upon the relativity of evil would also prescribe that one must face extreme danger unflinchingly, for after all, things are never as dire as they seem. In Baum's work, time and again, in all sorts of extremity, the idea is advanced that no matter how frightened one is, nothing is to be gained by causing a row about it. Imprisoned by the terrible Gargoyles (*Dorothy and the Wizard*), the Wizard says:

> '. . . there is no doubt they intend to kill us as dead as possible in a short time.'
>
> 'As dead as poss'ble would be pretty dead, wouldn't it?' asked Dorothy.
>
> 'Yes, my dear. But we have no need to worry about that just now. Let us examine our prison and see what it is like.'[41]

And when the Nome King and his allies are about to destroy all Oz, the Scarecrow says:

> 'Well . . . it certainly looks bad for Ozma, and all of us. But I believe it is wrong to worry over anything before it happens. It is surely time enough to be sad when our country is despoiled and our people made slaves. So let us not deprive ourselves of the few happy hours remaining to us.'
>
> 'Ah! that is real wisdom,' declared the Shaggy Man, approvingly. 'After we become really unhappy we shall regret these few hours that are left to us, unless we enjoy them to the utmost.'[42]

No other Baum characters, however, manage to outdo the downright cheerful resignation with which the protagonists of *The Sea Fairies* prepare to meet doom:

> Cap'n Bill now decided that they were lost. He drew Trot closer to his side and placed one arm around her.
>
> 'I can't save you, dear little mate,' he said sadly, 'but we've lived a long time together, an' now we'll die together. . . .
>
> '. . . never mind, Cap'n Bill; we've done the best we could, and we've had a fine time.'[43]

One of the drawbacks of extracting biographical data from fiction, on the premise that no writer ever performs at his profession without revealing himself, is that some of the personal data just as intriguingly fitted into the story as any other is not especially important. While Baum's religious-moral views seem very important indeed, especially since they have influenced so many tens of thousands of children, how about the fact that he was left-handed? There is no need to go to the biographies for this information; he mentions it several times. "Many of our greatest men are that way," asserts the Woodman. "To be left-handed is usually to be two-handed; the right-handed people are usually one-handed."[44]

Another borderline case comes to light with the references to alcohol—all of them affectionate—in his work. Was he a serious drinker? Certainly some of his earlier occupations were those often associated with either social or solitary drinking or both: journalism-printing for one, his interlude as a traveling salesman, whiling away boring evenings in smalltown hotels, for another.

That the heart condition led to medical prohibition against Baum's habit of chain-smoking cigars is noted in several sources.[45]   If the stricture was extended to alcohol, this fact is not provable by the same avenue, for there are no extant reminiscences of Baum the imbiber, or Baum the party cut-up. Yet there seems a strong possibility that he may have inserted his nostalgic fondness for liquor into his work when that fondness was frustrated in real life. (This in much the same way as he translated his frustrated yearning for a daughter into the creation of Dorothy, Betsy, Ozma, Trot—a whole fairyland dominated by young females, a topic to be discussed in a subsequent section.)

Ali Dubh the Arab, for instance, describing the secret contents of his golden flask (*John Dough*), says, "The Great Elixir? Ah, it is the Essence of Vitality, the Water of Life—the Greatest Thing in all the World!" With this to go on, then, we are hardly surprised, when the flask is confused with one containing Mme. Leontyne's rheumatism cure, to learn that she is overwhelmed by a euphoria suspiciously alcoholic. She feels lighter than air, floats across the room and up the stairs. Also, needless to say, her rheumatic pains disappear.

More pointed still is the story of the Cowardly Lion (*The Wizard*). Just as the Woodman, believing he needs a heart, displays extraordinary compassion, so the Lion, seeking courage, says on meeting the fierce Kalidahs: "We are lost, for they will surely tear us to pieces with their sharp claws. But stand close behind me, and I will fight them as long as I am alive." Even the Wizard tells the Lion, "You have plenty of courage,

I am sure. . . . All you need is confidence in yourself.
There is no living thing that is not afraid when it faces
danger. True courage is in facing danger when you are
afraid, and that kind of courage you have in plenty."
But the Lion is adamant. He wants "*the sort of courage
that makes one forget he is afraid.*"[46] So the Wizard—
the ultimate in confidence men because he provides self-
confidence—administers a dose from "a square green
bottle," a clear description of the very kind of bottle in
which Holland gin was sold in Baum's day. And if it
escapes the child reader what "Dutch courage" is, it is
no matter so far as the story is concerned.

Baum's most tactful allusion to this subject, however, may be when the Woodman, having rusted away
for years in the forest, says to his rescuers, "When I am
well oiled, I shall soon be all right again." The oil can
of the Woodman is thereafter given almost as prominent
a place in the stories as his ax.

This pun, intentional or not, was evidently not
entirely lost on earlier adult readers though it may have
escaped the attention of later ones. A pamphlet entitled
*A Tin Man's Joke Book; a Collection of Witty Sayings
and Funny Things* is among the Baumiana unearthed
by the IWOC and reported in the *Baum Bugle*. On the
pamphlet cover is a photograph of Dave Montgomery
in his costume as the Tin Woodman, but instead of the
usual oilcan he is holding a bottle suggestive of bourbon
or scotch. The *Bugle* comments that the bottle replaces
the oil can "for reasons known only to the publisher
or perhaps to Montgomery."

Or, it might be added, perhaps to Baum.

Even without the oil-alcohol connection, it should
scarcely be surprising that oil is a source of life in Oz.
Not only does the Woodman require frequent oiling,

but Tik-Tok is in the same situation in later books. One of the magic ingredients sought by Ojo (*Patchwork Girl*) is "a drop of oil from a live man's body." Water, on the other hand, is not necessarily such a source; it melts the witch, it stops Tik-Tok's clockwork when he falls in a fountain, it rusts the Woodman's joints. But to a writer whose fondly remembered upbringing was paid for by oil, the importance of oil in his reconstructed Eden can hardly be overestimated.

Among Baum enthusiasts it is generally accepted that if any Oz character represents Baum himself, it is the Wizard. One of the arguments is that the Wizard makes a false start by pretending to be something he is not (Baum made several false starts with occupations he was unable for various reasons to pursue), but in mid-career is set upon the right path when he settles down to learn how to perform real magic (something in the manner of Baum's presumably having finally recognized that writing for children was his "true" vocation).

There seems more evidence to indicate, however, that if any Oz character represents his author, it is the Woodman.

It would be pointless to attempt to identify Baum with the Woodman *only* because the Woodman's is the voice which utters the homilies. All the characters take their turns at that game, including the children. There are no "straight men" in the Oz group. One of the running arguments through the series, however, concerns the traditional rivalry of the head versus the heart. Baum, who correctly saw himself as a romantic in a rationalistic age, would be more appropriately linked with the heart in this instance, and it is the Woodman who champions that side of the discussion.

Also, it is the Woodman who of them all has spent

the most time standing idle. There is the implication that even the Scarecrow was made by the Munchkin farmer only a short time before Dorothy takes him off the pole in the cornfield. The Woodman on the other hand has stood in the forest through long years of uselessness until he is rescued by Dorothy, even as Baum (whose name in German, incidently, means "tree") was rescued from oblivion and pointless occupation by Dorothy and her popularity with readers.

And finally, it should be remembered, it is the Woodman who is looking for a new heart.

★　★　★　★　★

Baum died on May 6, 1919, at "Ozcot," his Hollywood home, among his prize-winning chrysanthemums and dahlias, his respectful family, and his voluminous correspondence with enthusiastic readers.

The manuscript on which he was then at work, *Glinda of Oz*, was edited by his son Frank and published posthumously. Notes and a fragmentary draft of still another story, *The Royal Book of Oz*, were presumably turned over by his publisher to a successor, Ruth Plumly Thompson, but no one seems to know exactly how much of this book was really Baum's work; the feeling is that the publisher may have exaggerated Baum's part in it to ease the transition. In any case Miss Thompson, as the new Royal Historian of Oz, brought it out, along with eighteen more Oz books in the years to follow.

But it was not only Baum's books which were kept alive after his death. The old dream of the successful "extravaganza" lived on as well.

Depending on point of view, it is either a resounding vindication of Baum's faith in Oz as dramatic material, or an enormous irony, that the 1939 celluloid *Wizard* poured more of a fortune back to its makers than the author would have imagined possible in terms of his own day, and went on to experience an existence as near to immortality as is possible in this world.

The film is not Baum, any more than Julian Mitchell's musical was Baum, but for different reasons. Actress Judy Garland, her inappropriate figure corseted to give a pale illusion of little-girlishness, presents a Dorothy completely alien to Baum's concept. Throughout, the production seesaws alarmingly between the sentimental and the grotesque, the very pitfalls Baum so scrupulously avoided in his first Oz book.

A *New Yorker* critic who claims to have "sat cringing" before MGM's *Wizard*, called the film "a stinkeroo" and complained about the lack of "imagination, good taste or ingenuity," and "the eye-straining Technicolor vulgarity," finishing off waspishly with: ". . . if Bert Lahr belongs in the Land of Oz, then so does Mae West."[47]

And yet if Baum were around today to give an opinion, there is not the slightest doubt it would be one of wholehearted approval, Judy Garland, Bert Lahr, and all. ("People will have what pleases them. . . .")

He never argued with success.

PART III

The Imaginary Continent: Baum's Fictional World

". . . when one is brought up to believe that beyond the horizon lie the perilous seas of faery lands forlorn, infested by demons, dragons, and men whose heads do grow beneath their shoulders, a tale that confirms this belief will find readier acceptance than one that refutes it."

L. Sprague DeCamp[1]

≫ ≫ OZ WAS NOT BROUGHT FORTH IN A VACUUM, OF COURSE. In an age of literary criticism which concerns itself more than most with generic connections between individual pieces of literature and groups of writings widely separated in time and space, Baum's fictional world is a veritable catchall for the historical, the mythic, and the folkloric. And as with most literature, some of these influences are included by the author quite consciously, while others spring fullblown out of the common heritage and either are or are not then modified by Baum to meet his own needs, or the needs of the story.

It is my purpose, in the following pages, to examine some of the sources of Oz and environs, and to see how they have helped shape Baum's work.

★　★　★　★　★

Certainly no human quest has beguiled men and nations with more persistence than the search for the faraway, legendary place. Usually an island in uncharted seas, but sometimes a continent, the fabulous land is the epitome of exoticism, but since it defies discovery, the game of speculation invites every man to project into the search his private daydreams.

Often the legend surrounding the undiscovered land

93

is one of magic, and frequently the magic is assumed to work in a way to veil the enchanted spot from human eyes, as with the mythical island of Hy-Brasil which, according to folklore, appears every seven years off the coast of Ireland. Hy-Brasil, which in Gaelic means "Isle of the Blest," is usually represented (just as the prototype is in Greek and Roman myth) as a resting place for the souls of the "chosen" on their journey to heaven, thus reinforcing the idea of the enchanted land as a place where there is no work, no care, no death, and suggesting too what is already obvious: that the *idea* of the existence of the legendary place is a far more important human need than the search itself, and the resultant uncovering of real places from time to time.

This point is made by Samuel Eliot Morison, who notes that even cartographers seek to preserve the illusions of the race if they can.

> Medieval maps covering the Atlantic, as time went on, became fairly crowded with islands big and small. Had they really existed, no ship could have sailed west from Europe without sighting one or more. Nor did the discovery of the Azores make any difference. One would suppose that these would have made map-makers say, 'This is it,' or 'These are them!' The Portuguese crown did give Brendanesque names to Flores and Corvo; but for a long time the nine Azores were simply spotted in as additions to the mythical archipelagoes.[2]

Among the best known and longest sought of the

legendary group was Antilia, which is often identified as the same place as the Isle of the Seven Cities, and is the basis of much Portuguese lore. According to some historians, Columbus—among many others—used charts showing the estimated position of Antilia, and had planned to stop there, if possible. Still other writers identify continental America itself as the "real" Antilia, which means "island opposite" (a land in the western hemisphere opposite Portugal would be America).

Another celebrated legendary place is St. Brendan's Isle, or St. Brendan's Land of Promise (source of the adjective "Brendanesque" in the passage from Morison), which usually appears in literature as still another version of Elysia, or as a prelapsarian paradise.

Baum of course would have come to maturity well before the dying-out of the magnificent tradition of search for the fabled land. So long as some part of the world remained unexplored, the chance existed that paradise would yet appear in some far location. One of Baum's strange characters, the Ork, a huge, bird-like quadruped which appears in *The Scarecrow of Oz*, echoes a sentiment which was still vitally a part of the nineteenth century:

'. . . it is astonishing how many little countries there are, hidden away in the cracks and
corners of this big globe of Earth. If one
travels, he may find some new country at
every turn, and a good many of them have
never yet been put upon the maps.'[3]

One might add, ". . . or taken off," for according to Morison, even the British Admiralty did not remove Hy-Brasil from its charts until 1873, and then cartographers were so reluctant to give up the legend that the corrupted name "Brazil" (which has no apparent etymological connection with the Gaelic "Brasil") was applied to an island-sized rock off Nova Scotia.[4]

But at this time too the tangled fable of the undiscovered land—a land lying always to westward, because of the westward drift of civilization—was growing brighter at the wick's end, for four centuries after the Hispanic discovery of America the magical territory could still be imagined to exist just beyond the American frontier. Maps showing the presumably unexplored Great American Desert, substantial though shrinking, were in use throughout the nineteenth century.

The fact that the Land of Oz is a self-contained enclave surrounded on all sides not by the sea but by impassable deserts suggests the undiscovered paradise which *might have been* an oasis at the core of the Great American Desert itself, if such a desert had existed on the scale once imagined by map-makers and explorers.

The Land of Oz, and also the Island of Yew, however, share a striking physical similarity to some of the mythical islands, tales of which kept mariners so hopefully scanning sixteenth and seventeenth century horizons. Oz has already been described as a rectangle; Yew is a perfect circle, divided "like a mince pie" into four kingdoms, with a fifth in the center. (Similarly, the four districts of Oz are centered by the Emerald City; the mythic significance of "quartering" and "centering" space will be considered later.) Antilia repeatedly appears on early maps as a rectangle, a contour it shares not only with Oz, but with the lesser known of the "real," charted mythical islands such as Satanzes, Surlenge, and Asent, which appear on many of the same maps as does Antilia. A squarish but not-so-regular island is the legendary Ymana, of the same group. Inevitably, on the other hand, Hy-Brasil is shown as perfectly circular. In some cases it is depicted as bifurcated by a strait, and in still others the strait is so wide that the land appears as a pair of semi-circular islands, flat sides facing. But in all cases the circularity itself is preserved.[5]

Quite another point of comparison, yet one almost as striking, is the direction one takes from the known world in order to reach the unknown. Is Oz also a westward land, as the location in a desert similar to America's desert implies? In the case of the first visit to Oz, the answer is not so easy. Dorothy arrives there when a cyclone, a midwest term for tornado, blasts her Kansas farmhouse from its foundation and bears it along on the updraft. True, because of the Rocky Mountain range, weather generally moves in an easterly direction on the Great Plains. But Dorothy's freak storm produces no sensation of direction except upward. The reader is never sure whether the updraft has deposited the Kansas house in a Baumian cloud-cuckoo-land which is literally in the clouds (or beyond), or if the structure has been set upon earth again, as the cyclone spends itself, but in some land far removed from Kansas.

On Dorothy's second visit (*Ozma*), however, she definitely strikes out on a westerly course. On a voyage to Australia she is swept into the sea, again during a storm, and washed ashore in the Land of Ev, from which she eventually proceeds to Oz. Striking out in the same direction on her third visit (*Dorothy and the Wizard*), she arrives in California from Kansas and tumbles through a crack in the earth, quake-caused, into the Land of the Mangaboos; she does not actually get all the way to Oz this time, however, without assistance from the thaumaturgic Ozma.

A new device (new in the Oz series; old in the sense that we are reminded of the Minotaur's Labyrinth, but without the beast), is used in the following story, *The Road to Oz*. Dorothy walks a short distance from her Kansas home and discovers that a familiar crossroads has been magically scrambled so that strange roads now lead in all possible directions. She chooses one by counting off seven from where she stands—and gets, of course, to Oz. But as in the adventure of the cyclone, no direction is hinted at.

Two other formulas for reaching Oz appear after *The Emerald City*, in which Dorothy, this time magically transported direct from her attic bedroom in Kansas, becomes a resident of the fairy country and so has no more need to find it. In *Tik-Tok* Betsy Bobbin is ship-wrecked in the Nonestic Ocean which, one feels, is very like the South Pacific. And in *The Scarecrow* Trot and Cap'n Bill are definitely along the Pacific offshore of California when they are swallowed up by a whirlpool and washed into a sea cavern, from which it is possible to proceed to Oz unassisted, at least unassisted by magic.

If Baum, who during his lifetime moved from New York to South Dakota, and from Chicago to that fabulous land of promise, Hollywood, gave conscious thought at all to the direction in which Oz lies (or even if he did not), he would scarcely have visualized his pastoral paradise in the industrial east or the chill Atlantic, for in Oz it is always like a summer in the country.

As for whether Oz is out of this world, or in it but not of it, evidence would seem to indicate the latter despite the early impression that the cyclone just might have dumped Dorothy beyond the clouds. Never-never lands may be, if not pin-pointed, at least given a general-

ized location, such as that of the Middle-earth of
Tolkien, or the Graustark of George Barr McCutcheon.[6]
Or they may exist entirely without reference to geography, like the Narnia of C. S. Lewis, approached in the
first Narnia book through the back wall of a wardrobe
in an English country house. The exact position of Oz
lies somewhere between these extremes. In *Dorothy
and the Wizard* the group scales Pyramid Mountain
(from the inside) and keeps an upward path thereafter,
assuming the earth's surface must be reached in order to
find Oz. And in *Tik-Tok* Ann Soforth's internal mono-
logue definitely places Oz among the countries of this
world.

> . . . it would be easy to conquer the Land of
> Oz and set herself up as Ruler in Ozma's place,
> if she but had an Army to do it with. After-
> ward she could go out into the world and
> conquer other lands, and then perhaps she
> could find a way to the moon, and conquer
> that.[7]

As his series went on, Baum enhanced the already
substantial belief in the existence of Oz not by any
more explication of its whereabouts—indeed, that given
here is about all there is—but by providing an increasingly comprehensive idea of the contours and peculiar-
ities of its geography once one is there. The most
inspired of the steps taken in this direction is a document printed on the endpapers of *Tik-Tok* labeled, "A
map of the marvelous Land of Oz showing its great
protective desert barriers, and many of the celebrated
and magical countries which lie beyond the parched
sands." The drawing shows nearly a score of other

fairylands on the outer periphery of the surrounding desert, lands mentioned in stories written, appropriately, mostly outside the Oz cycle. The map also shows the shore of the Nonestic Ocean, the sea in which the greater fairy continent lies. None of the other fairylands, incidently, has the regularity of shape (either rectangular or circular) discussed earlier in connection with Oz and Yew. The Land of Ev, Noland, Merryland, Hiland and Loland, Ripple Land, the Vegetable Kingdom, the Isle of Phreex—all are as random as the shapes of Texas, or Ohio, or California. Only the Isle of Pingaree is roughly circular, but the written descriptions (*Rinkitink in Oz*) indicate it has none of the refinements (such as the four kingdoms) of Yew.

(Unfortunately, when Baum did this mapping of Oz and generously credited the job to the Woggle-Bug, his ambidexterous pen slipped so that he showed the Munchkin Country in the west, the Winkie Country in the east. It is clear in the text that Dorothy first lands in the east of Oz, in the Munchkin land, and her journey there at least is definitely westward. Baum's resourceful publisher, aware that anything is possible in Oz, used the map as it was submitted, but exchanged east and west points on the diagrammatic compass.)

In a way, Oz has one more thing in common with the fabulous lands of history, especially the invisible-visible Hy-Brasil. When Baum chose to end his series with *The Emerald City*, the method used was to render his magic land undetectable to the ordinary human eye. Unlike Hy-Brasil, however, Oz was not to undergo periodic visibility, but was to be hidden from view forever, the enchantment working two ways. At least readers of *The Patchwork Girl*, which came next, learn that to the people living in Oz, the rest of the world is

no longer visible either. When Oz residents reach the
borders of their territory—a point from which in former
times they had a vista of the burning sands—they now
see "nothing." However, still later we find that forever
is too long a time even for Ozian enchantments to
endure. Betsy Bobbin has no difficulty seeing Oz when
she arrives, nor do Trot and Cap'n Bill, both cases which
occur in still-later stories.

For whenever and wherever life is made especially
    Baum's plot to scrap the series was abortive, as we
have already seen. Nye observes that ". . . he was
driven back to Oz by the demands of his readers and,
one suspects, his own unconscious inclinations."[8] And
while Baum did have his money losses to cover, and Oz
represented one sure way to pay the bills (as we have
seen in a prior section), this circumstance doesn't obviate
the validity of the latter half of Nye's comment.

For whenever and wherever life is made especially
painful for whatever reason—political, economic, psy-
chological or physiological—visions of eden-utopia recur
individually and collectively with increasing fervor and
clarity of detail. Maud Bodkin describes this process in
some detail:

> ". . . The blossoming sunlit garden, the
> blessed spot, green and fountainous, which
> rises before the inward eye of poet and travel-
> ler alike, in times of weariness and hardship,
> appears very simply related to the needs of
> our nature. . . . Amid various circumstances
> of painful tension, the image of a Paradise of
> calm and soft luxuriance, 'Where life is easiest
> for man,' fulfils the requirement of [Freud's]
> pleasure-principle, as offering a condition of
> subjective release. Heaven, as the Persian poet

conceived it—the moment of time when I am
tranquil—is an ideal in apparent harmony with
a regressive trend toward irresponsible infancy,
or even toward pre-natal peace.[9]

In this sense, as well as that of an offspring of
cartographical curiosities of past centuries, the Land of
Oz is familiar territory. If one looks upon it as this
condition of innocence and innocent wish-fulfillment,
the Golden Age, the utopia which is the "realization"
of the human dream of perfection, it becomes immediately apparent that the appropriate furniture is all there
and in place: eternal youth and immortality, peace,
plenty, a just and wise government, the certain triumph
of truth and goodness, an elevated and pacified animal
kingdom, the fruitful Garden, the dazzling city.
    In apprehending and expressing the archetype of
the Golden Age, various degrees of sophistication are
of course possible, from a simple concept of a time and
place where all things are provided and nothing de-
manded (the condition which exists in the womb, or
the Garden before the Fall), to a complete welfare state
which offers political answers to the besetting problems
of social man.
    Baum's eden, characteristically, is a pastiche, draw-
ing upon the notion of the ideal society as well as the
infantile version of the perfect sanctuary.

There were no poor people in the Land of Oz,
because there was no such thing as money,
and all property of every sort belonged to the
Ruler. The people were her children, and she
cared for them. Each person was given freely
by his neighbors whatever he required for his

people of our own world. There were all sorts
of queer characters among them, but not a
single one who was evil, or who possessed a
selfish or violent nature. They were peaceful,
kind-hearted, loving and merry, and every
inhabitant adored the beautiful girl who ruled
them, and delighted to obey her every command.[10]

For purposes of plot, Baum was soon forced to
compromise this last statement. *Tik-Tok*, for instance
begins with a projected revolution led by Queen Ann
Soforth of Oogaboo, a remote part of Oz (but nonetheless a part), and in *Magic of Oz* Ugu the Shoemaker,
a disaffected Ozite, attempts to undermine Ozma's rule
by stealing all her magic and that of Glinda, to name
just two cases.

Further, in *The Patchwork Girl* it turns out that
while production methods in Oz may be working splendidly, distribution facilities occasionally leave something
to be desired. At the beginning of the story Ojo and
his uncle, living in a remote forest of the Munchkin
country, face starvation after they pick the last ripe
loaf from the bread tree in their yard. "Of course,"
says Ojo, "no one starves in the Land of Oz. . . . There
is plenty for everyone, you know; only, if it isn't just
where you happen to be, you must go where it is."[11]

The effect of such exceptions to the norm, however, is to strengthen rather than diminish the high
degree of credibility already established by the insistence
on such specificities as the map. For on every possible
occasion, Baum piles detail upon detail. Besides explaining the workings of his utopian government, before
the cycle is over he has—among other things—accounted

use, which is as much as any one
ably desire. Some tilled the lands
great crops of grain, which was divided
among the entire population, so that ai.
enough. There were many tailors and dre
makers and shoemakers and the like, who
made things that any who desired them might
wear. Likewise there were jewelers who made
ornaments for the person, which pleased and
beautified the people, and these ornaments
also were free to those who asked for them.
Each man and woman, no matter what he or
she produced for the good of the community,
was supplied by the nieghbors with food and
clothing and a house and furniture and ornaments and games. If by chance the supply
ever ran short, more was taken from the great
storehouses of the Ruler, which were afterward filled up again when there was more of
any article than the people needed.

Everyone worked half the time and played
half the time, and the people enjoyed the
work as much as they did the play, because
it is good to be occupied and to have work to
do. There were no cruel overseers set to
watch them, and no one to rebuke them or to
find fault with them. So each one was proud
to do all he could for his friends and neighbors, and was glad when they would accept
the things he produced.

Oz being a fairy country, the people were,
of course, fairy people; but that does not
mean that all of them were very unlike the

for the origin of Oz (giving not one but two possible cosmogonies), commented with anthropological zeal upon the eccentricities of inhabitants to be found in outlying specialized colonies and elsewhere, and disclosed census figures for its single urban area.[12]

> It [the Emerald City] has nine thousand, six hundred and fifty-four buildings, in which lived fifty-seven thousand three hundred and eighteen people, up to the time my story opens.[13]

Similar concern for credibility is shown in the no-death rule: "No disease of any sort was ever known among the Ozites, and so no one ever died, *unless he met with an accident that prevented him from living.*"[14] The conditional item in this statement is for the most part a way of accommodating after the fact to what has already occurred in the first book rather than a preparation for what is to come, for few accidents occur in later stories. However, in *The Wizard*, before the author himself had stabilized the norms of his fictional world, the Wicked Witch of the East is "killed" by Dorothy's house, and Dorothy herself "melts" the Wicked Witch of the West as the result of an "accident."

In the same story it is implied that the Woodman's parents have died, since he says he lived with them "as long as they were alive." And on the first journey to the Emerald City the Woodman kills forty attacking wolves by chopping off their heads with his ax, while the Scarecrow twists the necks of forty crows "until at last all were lying dead beside him." Then a swarm of stinging bees is sent to attack the party, but the bees break their stingers on the Woodman without penetrating his metal skin. "And as bees cannot live when their stings are broken, that was the end of the black bees. . . ." Meeting the same awful fate are the kalidahs, beasts with bodies like bears, heads like tigers. When *they* attack, the Woodman deflects their trail over a log bridge and they are "dashed to pieces on the sharp rocks" at the bottom of the ravine.

An even grislier note is struck when the Cowardly Lion becomes hungry and withdraws into the woods for a while. Later no one questions him about what he has had for lunch. However, the Hungry Tiger of succeeding books is prohibited by his own troublesome conscience from devouring any living creature—he is said to relish plump babies—and must subsist on porridge. And Ojo is thwarted in his quest for the wing of a yellow butterfly, which he must have to bring his uncle back to life after he has been magically petrified, because of the stipulation that no animal, no matter how small, can be killed in Oz and by law may not be tortured or maimed.

This flight of imagination is extended even to pestiferous insects. "If a fly lights on his [an Ozite's] body, he doesn't rudely brush it off, but asks it politely to find some other resting place. Usually it begs his pardon and goes away." And mosquitoes don't bite people because "they are well fed and taken care of." Yet in the second book, *The Land of Oz*, Mombi raises swine, which implies a harsher fate for some animals.

This same idea, that the rule of immortality does not after all always apply to animals in the same way as to human beings, is supported by the news (in *The Emerald City*, only forty-one pages after the assertion that "no disease of any sort was ever known among the Ozites . . .") that one of Billina's chicks "took cold at

Ozma's birthday party and died of the pip. . . ."[15]
So chickens are notorious for their high mortality rate
even in the Land of Oz. And any child of a chicken
farmer would see this as absolutely plausible.

One of the rare instances (after the first book) of
those accidents which prevent people from living *seems*
to be reported in *The Road to Oz* by the Woodman, who
says, ". . . the crooked Sorcerer who invented the
magic Powder [of life] fell down a precipice and was
killed."[16] But the Woodman is misinformed; the same
crooked magician turns up later in *The Patchwork Girl*,
alive and well, still making the powder.

In maintaining to whatever degrec throughout the
Oz cycle this no-death rule, Baum quite obviously had
to face a problem familiar to other writers about im-
mortals, among them John Milton in "Paradise Lost."
Not all critics of course feel as strongly as Cleanth
Brooks when he suggests that ". . . the absurdity of a
battle in which contestants cannot be killed is a flaw in
Milton's great poem. . . ."[17] But the problem remains.

Although Baum has partially protected himself
with his clause about accidents preventing one from
living (which would surely cover battle wounds if
need be) from being placed in Milton's position, he has
given the matter considerable thought, as is evident
from his comments from time to time. These comments, however, are for the most part reserved for the
later books. Early, in *Land*, when the army of girls
declares war on the Emerald City and Tip cautions
General Jinjur: "Many of you will be slain!" she takes
refuge in the code of chivalry: "What man would
oppose a girl, or dare to harm her?"[18] But there is no
danger in any case since the "standing army" of Oz at
that time consists of a single soldier with a blunderbuss
he does not know how to fire.

In *The Emerald City*, however, the issue is confronted more seriously. The would-be invaders discuss the troublesome fact that they cannot kill their immortal enemies and so lay plans to capture and enslave them. The device "works," for there is no loss of tension and interest in the story.

A more depressing exploration of the subject occurs in *Tik-Tok* when the Army of Oogaboo is attacked by the Rak, and Private Files reminds his trembling superior officers that ". . . we people of Oogaboo, which is part of the fairyland of Oz, cannot be killed." But Captain Buttons inquires, ". . . if the Rak catches us, and chews us up into small pieces, and swallows us—what will happen then?" Files declares: "Then each small piece will still be alive." Understandably, though, the officers are not reassured by this. "A hamburger steak is a hamburger steak, whether it is alive or not!"[19] The conversation anticipates a speech by the Nome King in *The Magic of Oz*: "True . . . the Oz people cannot be killed, but they can be cut into small pieces, and while every piece will still be alive, we can scatter the pieces around so that they will be quite helpless."[20] It is with something almost of shock, too, that we find, in *The Patchwork Girl*: "The little Munchkin boy had never heard of any person dying in the Land of Oz, but he knew one could suffer a great deal of pain."[21]

Perhaps the device which in the end contributes most to the continuing suspense in tales of the near-battles in Oz, however, has less to do with prospective maiming and scattering of bodies than with the ever-present thematic vein of absolute pacifism. The reader is already thoroughly acquainted with the idea that in Oz one doesn't fight, because fighting doesn't solve anything. He knows that despite the talk of mayhem, there will be none, since Ozites never compromise their principles. What then will be the ruse which defeats the enemy?

The girl army is ultimately vanquished by a comic-strip strategy: the Scarecrow turns loose a number of field mice he has earlier hidden away for this purpose in his straw interior. Ann Soforth's expedition against Oz is defeated at the outset when the road from Oogaboo to the Emerald City is magically manipulated so that it leads in another direction entirely. The massive invasion (*Emerald City*) by the Nomes and allies actually does take place—up to a point. But the tunnel the enemy has drilled under the impassable desert has its egress in Ozma's palace garden, conveniently near the Forbidden Fountain. The fountain emits the magical Waters of Oblivion which, when taken internally, cause the mind to become blank. As the invaders emerge, hot and dusty from the long trip through the subterranean corridor, they drink, and forget their plan of attack. Ozma has said, "I would like to discover a plan to save ourselves without fighting," and so she does. (Like the experience of Mme. Leontyne who drinks the Elixir, the resulting "oblivion" of the Nomes is not without its alcoholic overtones.)

The real problem with Baum in this area, however, is that once the reader becomes, partway through the series, thoroughly conditioned to the provisos for both immortality and pacifism as a solution to all difficulty, some of the contingent rules in Oz begin to seem incongruous if not incompatible with these provisos. It may come as a surprise, for instance, that in Baum's paradise there is capital punishment, or at least the machinery for accomplishing it. In *The Road to Oz* Dorothy says, "But I thought no one ever died in Oz," to which the

Woodman replies, "Nor do they; although if one is bad, he may be condemned and killed by the good citizens."[22]

Oz justice in connection with this law usually turns out to be tempered with reluctance, however. In *The Lost Princess* the Lavender Bear sentences Cayke the Cookie Cook and the Frog Man for trespassing in Bear Center:

> 'I condemn you both to death, the execution to take place ten years from this hour!'
>
> 'But we belong to the land of Oz, where no one ever dies,' Cayke reminded him.
>
> 'Very true,' said the King. 'I condemn you to death merely as a matter of form. It sounds quite terrible, and in ten years we shall have forgotten all about it. . . .'[23]

Similarly Glinda, in *The Land of Oz*, tells Mombi, ". . . unless you tell me all that you know, I will certainly put you to death." But the Tin Woodman demurs. "Oh, no! Don't do that. . . . It would be an awful thing to kill anyone—even old Mombi!" Glinda clears the air, if not the prisoner, with a much more tactful version of the ultimatum: ". . . it is merely a threat. . . . I shall not put Mombi to death, because she will prefer to tell me the truth."[24]

Far more serious, with overtones of a judicial system quite alien to the standards of most utopias, is the trial of Eureka in *Dorothy and the Wizard*, for it is quite clear from the beginning that if the kitten is found guilty she really will be put to death. Moreover the situation early hints of double jeopardy:

'What will happen if she is guilty?' asked Dorothy.

'She must die,' answered the Princess.

'Nine times?' enquired the Scarecrow.

'As many times as is necessary,' was the reply.[25]

And yet reluctance is shown here too when the author himself intrudes to observe:

> . . . whenever an appeal is made to law sor-
> row is almost certain to follow—even in a
> fairyland like Oz. But it must be stated that
> the people of that land were generally so well-
> behaved that there was not a single lawyer
> among them, and it had been years since any
> Ruler had sat in judgment upon an offender
> of the law.[26]

Also, it is strictly on the prisoner's behalf that the affair is turned into a kangaroo court, with the Wizard, a witness, expressing strong anti-capital punishment sentiments in his advice to the Woodman, who is acting as defense attorney:

> 'My friend, it is your duty to defend the
> white [sic] kitten and try to save her, but I
> fear you will fail because Eureka has long
> wished to eat a piglet, to my certain knowl-
> edge, and my opinion is that she has been
> unable to resist the temptation. Yet her dis-
> grace and death would not bring back the
> piglet, but only serve to make Dorothy un-

happy.   So I intend to prove the kitten's innocence by a trick.'[28]

It is to *The Patchwork Girl*, however, that we must turn for Baum's most detailed theory of law and punishment. Ojo, who needs a six-leaved clover for the magic formula which will restore his petrified uncle to life, is told there is a law against picking one in Oz. But "he could really see no harm in picking a six-leaved clover, if he found one, and in spite of what the Shaggy Man had said he considered Ozma's law to be unjust."[28] So Ojo picks the clover, thinking he has been unobserved, but Glinda's foolproof surveillance system (a magic book in which is written everything that goes on everywhere, as it happens) finds him out. He is arrested upon his entry into the Emerald City, handcuffed, and robed in a sheet-like costume suggestive of the Klan. The purpose of this costuming is two-fold: to provide Ojo with anonymity before the trial, and to show his status as prisoner. He is then removed to the only jail in Oz and received there by the turnkey, who reacts somewhat strangely for a penal officer, even one in Oz: "Goodness me! A Prisoner at last."

The prison is not only comfortable, it is posh. "The walls were paneled with plates of gold decorated with gems of great size and many colors, and upon the tiled floor were soft rugs delightful to walk upon. . . . In one place a case filled with books stood against the wall and elsewhere Ojo saw a cupboard containing all sorts of games."[29]   None of the doors is locked but Ojo decides that "if his jailer was willing to trust him in this way he would not betray her trust, and moreover a hot supper was being prepared for him and his prison was very pleasant and comfortable."[30]   By way of explanation, Tollydiggle, the motherly jailer, says:

> 'We consider a prisoner unfortunate. He is
> unfortunate in two ways—because he has done
> something wrong and because he is deprived
> of liberty. Therefore we should treat him
> kindly, because of his misfortune, for other-
> wise he would become hard and bitter and
> would not be sorry he had done wrong. Ozma
> thinks that one who has committed a fault
> did so because he was not strong and brave;
> therefore she puts him in prison to make him
> strong and brave.'[31]

She further reassures Ojo about what is in store for
him in the way of punishment:

> 'Isn't one punished enough in knowing he has
> done wrong? . . . When you are tried and
> found guilty, you will be obliged to make
> amends in some way. I don't know just what
> Ozma will do to you, because this is the first
> time one of us has broken a Law; but you may
> be sure she will be just and merciful. Here in
> the Emerald City people are too happy and
> contented ever to do wrong; but perhaps you
> came from some faraway corner of our land,
> and having no love for Ozma carelessly broke
> one of her laws.'

Meanwhile, Scraps, trying to protect her friend Ojo,
takes the incriminating clover from his basket and hides
it in a gold vase at the palace. But the all-seeing eye of
Glinda scores again; the clover is produced at the trial.

Ojo pleads guilty, but still insists on his right to civil disobedience: ". . . it seemed to me a foolish law, unjust and unreasonable. Even now I can see no harm in picking a six-leaved clover." To which Ozma replies, "I suppose a good many laws seem foolish to those people who do not understand them, but no law is ever made without some purpose, and that purpose is usually to protect all the people and guard their welfare."[32]

She goes on to explain that the law was made to prevent magic being practised in the land without her consent, ". . . so you see the Law was not a foolish one, but wise and just; and, in any event, it is wrong to disobey a law."[33]

Ojo, not surprisingly, is forgiven by Ozma, but from all this we learn several more sobering things about law in Oz. A prisoner is presumed guilty and the burden of proving a negative is on the side of the defense (true in the trials both of Ojo and Eureka the Pink Kitten). Loftiness of motive is not always a mitigating circumstance after all. And a law, no matter how seemingly unjust, is unassailable. Furthermore, the evidence-gathering methods of the state are more like *1984* than 1913. The fact that Baum's ideas of penology are somewhat advanced for his time hardly makes up for the harshness of the rest. After all, Oz *is* Utopia.

On the other hand, when the group in *Tik-Tok* is thrown by the Nomes down the Forbidden Tube, which leads through the center of the earth to an antipodal fairyland, they face a law there which says anyone coming through the Tube must be tortured nine days and ten nights and then thrown back into the Tube. But the Private Citizen (the only non-royal dweller in the land, he rules over the fairy kings and queens) decrees: "It is wise to disregard laws when they conflict with justice, and it seems that you . . . did not disobey the laws willingly. . . ."[34] Though this land is not Oz, the concept seems more appropriate to Baum the Relativist, whom we met in the previous section.

Quite apart from its failures to live up to utopian standards, Baum's penal system has strong echoes of the Samuel Butler formula presented in *Erewhon*, first published in 1872, though the differences between the two probably far outweigh the likenesses. In Butler's utopia the vigorous good health of the people is explained by the strict enforcement of a law demanding the incarceration of the sick. This threat of being severely dealt with has a salubrious effect upon hypochondriacs and malingerers. Meanwhile, criminals are treated with the utmost tenderness; it is the *victims* of crimes who are punished under Erewhonian law:

> . . . if a man forges a check, or sets his house on fire, or robs with violence from the person, or does any other such things as are criminal in our own country, he is either taken to a hospital and most carefully tended at the public expense, or if he is in good circumstances, he lets it be known to all his friends that he is suffering from a severe fit of immorality, just as we do when we are ill, and they come and visit him with great solicitude, and inquire with interest how it all came about, what symptoms first showed themselves, and so forth,—questions which he will answer with perfect unreserve; for bad conduct, though considered no less deplorable than illness with ourselves, and as unquestionably indicating something seriously wrong with the individual

who misbehaves, is nevertheless held to be the
result of either pre-natal or post-natal mis-
fortune. . . . Ill luck of any kind, or even ill
treatment at the hands of others, is considered
an offense against society, inasmuch as it
makes people uncomfortable to hear of it.
Loss of fortune, therefore, or loss of some
dear friend on whom another was much
dependent, is punished hardly less severely
than physical delinquency.[35]

As we have seen, there is no illness in Oz either,
though it has been banished by another kind of decree.
Criminals are treated much the same, however. The
narrator of *Erewhon*, arrested upon his illegal entry into
the country and detained for investigation, describes a
sumptuous detention facility not unlike the jail in Oz.
Baum, familiar with Butler or not, perhaps coincides
most closely with the other utopia-creator in his emphasis upon rapid and sympathetic rehabilitation of the
person who has undergone a moral lapse. This at least
is a thoroughly utopian convention and seems as appropriate to Oz as to Erewhon.

A more natural concomitant of the no-death rule
in Oz (more natural, that is, than capital punishment
and jailing of criminal offenders) is the fact that Ozites
do not age, though birthdays are always celebrated with
gusto. The no-aging is made explicit in connection with
the recounting of the second cosmogony (in *The Tin
Woodman*) and the two subjects turn out to be more
closely linked than might first appear.

Oz was not always a fairyland, I am told.
Once it was much like other lands, except it

was shut in by a dreadful desert of sandy wastes that lay all around it, thus preventing its people from all contact with the rest of the world.   Seeing this isolation, the fairy band of Queen Lurline, passing over Oz while on a journey, enchanted the country and so made it a Fairyland.   And Queen Lurline left one of her fairies to rule this enchanted Land of Oz, and then passed on and forgot all about it.

From that moment no one in Oz ever died. Those who were old remained old; those who were young and strong did not change as years passed them by; the children remained children always, and played and romped to their hearts' content, while all the babies lived in their cradles and were tenderly cared for and never grew up.   So people in Oz stopped counting how old they were in years, for years made no difference in their appearance and could not alter their station.   They did not get sick, so there were no doctors among them.   Accidents might happen to some, on rare occasions, it is true, and while no one could die naturally, as other people do, it was possible that one might be totally destroyed. . . .[36]

Again, however, awkwardnesses are immediately apparent.   The Crooked Magician in *The Patchwork Girl*, explaining about Ojo to the glass cat, says: "He is now small because he is young.   With more years he will grow big and become as tall as Unc Nunkie . . . it is Nature's magic, which is more wonderful than any art known to man."[37]

More important, though, is the story of Ozma herself. In *Land* she (as Tip) is described not as having been deputized by Queen Lurline to rule over Oz, but as having been a baby brought up by the witch Mombi. At the end of this book and in the other early work she is seen as a child approximately the age of Dorothy, "neither older nor larger than Dorothy herself."[38] Later (*The Tin Woodman*), and with no forewarning, it is revealed that Ozma has grown, but Dorothy has not. "To judge Ozma of Oz by the standards of the world, you would think her very young—perhaps fourteen or fifteen years of age—yet for years she had ruled the Land of Oz and had never seemed a bit older. Dorothy appeared much younger than Ozma. She had been a little girl when she first came to the Land of Oz, and she was a little girl still, and would never seem to be a day older while she lived in this wonderful fairyland."[39]

The confusion stems from the same auctorial manipulations which led also to the change in the story of the origin of Oz: Baum had been slowly revising the norms of his fictional world from the first book onward, and he wanted his girl ruler and her history to fit more gracefully into these norms. So he literally revised Ozma too.

In other words, the first story of Oz's past (*Land*) assumes the country has always been a fairyland. Princess Ozma is the daughter of Pastoria, "the first king of Oz," who has been, when the story opens, "dead and gone" for several years. In an effort to gain the throne of the Emerald City, which he in fact occupies when the book first opens, the Wizard of Oz kidnaps the baby princess on the death of the reigning king, and delivers her to the witch Mombi who by magic changes the child into a boy, Tip. Tip's re-transformation and rightful ascension to the throne climax the book.

The later story of how Oz came into existence upon the whim of Lurline (who is presumably some kind of super fairy queen out of the cosmos; the name in this and other forms appears elsewhere in fairy mythology, including the German, where "Lurlei" is an alternate form of "Lorelei"), on the other hand, violates no rules, since Ozma's succession does not depend on the unaccountable death of a father in a country where there is no death, and it expunges the record of the Wizard as wrongdoer. In later stories his behavior is impeccable; even his identity as a humbug, one of the central points of the first book, is all but forgotten. He is everybody's friend, a kind of guru among gurus.

But most useful of all to the new concept of Oz, the promotion of Ozma to maturity—at least partial maturity—enhances her maternal role. For while the female dominance so indispensable to Baum's womb-like world resides in Dorothy in the first book, it undergoes not so much a transfer to Ozma as a diffusion among the several female principals, of which Ozma is by far the most important. So that in later books it is the hand of Ozma—or sometimes Glinda, her confidante and mentor—that rocks the cradle of Oz, while Dorothy surrenders some of her leadership but retains much of the courage, practicality, and "little-girlishness" which are after all the real bases of her claim upon the reader.

Still another possible influence leading to Baum's decision to change his girl-child queen to an older, post-pubescent though still virgin ruler is the Graustark series by George Barr McCutcheon, mentioned earlier. The first Graustark story, *Graustark: The Story of a Love Behind a Throne*,[40] was published in 1901, a year after *The Wizard* but seventeen years before Ozma

emerges as an adolescent in *The Tin Woodman*, 1918.
Baum's fellow-Chicagoan earned a substantial (though
not so enduring) popularity for Graustark, which shares
certain obvious similarities with Oz. Both are fabulous
principalities ruled by young girls who remain inviolate;
in the first volumes of each series the story moves from
everyday circumstances in the United States and then
makes the jump to a mythical land. Baum and
McCutcheon, registered Democrats both, show in their
writing a deep reverence for royalty. While Yetive of
Graustark, who is twenty-one, and Ozma combine royal
hauteur with innocence to approximately the same
degree, it is true that the McCutcheon heroine is a bit
more "flesh and blood," while Ozma takes all honors
for sticky-sweet remoteness. At the same time, Baum
remains generally the better writer. Graustark becomes
slightly ridiculous to the reader from the moment the
hero, Grenfall Lorry, begins pursuing the princess,
traveling incognito as "Miss Guggenslocker." Oz is never
ridiculous; moreover, it is easy to believe Oz exists, but
not Graustark, even though the latter is more or less
definitely located for the reader "in the Alps." The
discussion of its whereabouts anticipates the Ork's
speech[41] with rare fidelity:

> '. . . If these people live in such a place, why,
> it is to be found, of course. Any railroad
> guide-book can locate this land of mystery.
> There are so many infernal little kingdoms
> and principalities over here [in Europe] that
> it would take a lifetime to get 'em all straight-
> ened out in one's head. . . .'[42]

Inevitably, in any discussion of sources used by
Baum, one must sooner or later confront the funda-

mental question of the source of the word "Oz" itself. The trouble with such speculation is that there are far too many possible answers, many of them already proposed by other writers. "I am Oz, the Great and Terrible," says the Wizard to Dorothy when she arrives in his august presence. Which surely calls up Shelleyan echoes of "My name is Ozymandias, king of kings." Baum would have been familiar with Shelley certainly, but then so was he—and probably to a greater degree— with the Bible, in which the Land of Uz is listed as the homeland of Job. And while the author could scarcely be considered a linguist, the fact remains that the Hebrew word "oz" (pronounced with a long "o") means "strength."

As recently as 1967, in a book column of the *Saturday Review*, Baum's own fanciful anecdote on this subject was still being retailed. He had a three-drawer file cabinet, the story goes, labeled A-G, H-N, and O-Z. While ad libbing a fairy tale to neighborhood children one day, Baum was asked by a listener, "What was the name of this land, Mr. Baum?" To which the author is supposed to have responded, as his eye fell by sheer chance on the bottom drawer of the cabinet, "The Land of Oz."

Daniel P. Mannix[43] has traced this anecdote to an interview Baum gave the *Los Angeles Mirror* January 27, 1904. "Well, I have a little cabinet file on my desk just before me. I was thinking and wondering about a title and had settled on 'wizard' as part of it. My gaze was caught by the gilt letters on the three drawers of the cabinet. . . . My eyes rested on the last drawer and Oz furnished the missing link for my title." For more than one reason this explanation has to be spurious, an improvisation after the fact, reflecting a skill Baum is well known to have exercised outside his books as well as in. It is a matter of record that Baum turned in the manuscript which later became *The Wizard* with nothing about "Wizard" or "Oz" in its title. The book was to be called *The Emerald City*, a title eventually attached to the sixth book. It was only after a number of editorial conferences that someone (not necessarily Baum) came up first with *The Wonderful Wizard*, and finally with *The Wonderful Wizard of Oz*.

In any case, Baum wouldn't have answered "Oz" to a child's casual query about the fairyland, as in the *Saturday Review* version of the legend. For, as Jay Delkin points out in a recent essay,[44] "Oz" in the original story is the proper name for the Wizard, not the land. The phrase "Wizard *of* Oz" is used only in the eventual title of the first book, never in the text, which has several references to "the Wizard Oz." Dorothy does indeed exclaim, "This must be the Land of Oz," but she is clearly referring to the Emerald City and immediate environs, where she has been told the Wizard lives. Only in succeeding books does "Oz" finally become the name of the entire fairy country.

Jack Snow, an earlier writer about Baum and himself the author of two Oz series titles, had in 1954 called the filing cabinet yarn "too glib" and remarked, "I don't think Baum's mind worked the filing cabinet way."[45] But then Snow goes on to suggest an even more unlikely source of the word: Baum, "a great lover of Dickens," might have dropped the "B" from Dickens' pen-name (Boz). The trouble with this is that Dickens made it clear to readers that "Boz" was a childish mispronunciation of "Mose," or "Moses." And it is common knowledge that Baum pronounced his fairyland with a short "o." For good measure, Snow has an

alternative speculation, this one with more weight perhaps. Recalling that in his foreword to *A New Wonderland* Baum wrote that he liked tales which caused the
reader to react with "Ohs" and "Ahs," Snow points out
that the word "Oz" may be pronounced either "Ohs,"
or "Ahs."

But for the sake of saying a final word on a subject
for which no final word is really possible, we should
keep in mind that Baum was fond of two-letter combina-
tions as names for his settings. Perhaps almost any odd-
sounding syllable would do—Mo, Ev, Oz, Ix. The first
might be a reversal of the Buddhist sacred syllable
"Om," (or "AUM") from the Sanskrit, and the second
might be meant to suggest the word "everywhere."
As for "Ix," that is easiest of all: a Roman numeral
which is a multiple of the magical number three. But
then who knows what stories Baum might himself tell
about the sources of these names? Only one thing is
certain: his explanations would be far more elaborate
than anything that anyone else could concoct after the
fact.

Up to now in this section, with a few exceptions,
we have been considering the historical bits and pieces
which went into the making of Oz: the legends of lost
or fabulous lands, the utopian elements, the published
works of other writers who may or may not have exerted
real influence upon Baum's writing, but in either case
do provide likenesses too marked to ignore. It is a
many-sided subject to which we shall return. Meanwhile, however, it is important to remember that for
all its identifiable twentieth-century Yankee attitudes
and ingredients, Oz is first and last constructed of the
stuff of the primitive unconscious, the darkly glittering
building materials of all myth and fairy tale.

The very structure of the land, for instance, four provinces contingent upon a common center, owes its arrangement to one of mankind's earliest concepts, the quartering of space; and though quartering becomes a mythic motif which weaves in and out of the fairy lore of both oriental and occidental cultures, Mary Barnard points out that it was probably originally simply a device for survival based upon one of primitive man's first observations of nature.[46] Even a preliterate intelligence would have no difficulty in noting the stable directions East and West, since sunrise and sunset mark them, and at night the most conspicuous directions are north in the northern hemisphere, south in the southern, because of the stars that wheel above the horizon at these points but do not set. But because the directions themselves are abstract ideas, the most obvious secondary step in all cultures has been to assign some usable symbolism, a god or a color, to more easily convey the abstract. Hence the mythologies in which space is supported north, east, south, and west by four caryatids, dwarfs, or giants, one of the oldest systems being the Egyptian, with its Hawk-headed god of the West, the Ape-headed god in the North, the Man-headed god of the South, and the Jackal-headed god of the East. Assigning colors to the directions is another quite common device, but according to Barnard, although directional colors are found from Tibet to the American Southwest and Central America, no two neighboring tribes agree on the particular hues to be assigned.

The four sectors of Oz, all roughly isosceles triangles, are the blue Munchkin country of the East, the red Quadling country of the south, the yellow Winkie country of the West, and the purple Gillikin country of the north. The Emerald City is, unsurprisingly, green, but it is clear that the city represents also a combining and consolidating of the other colors and directions. For one thing it is the seat of government; all Ozites, Quadlings, Gillikins, Winkies, and Munchkins, are loyal to Ozma even though they may have a local ruler as well. The Tin Woodman fulfills this role in the Winkie country where he is "emperor," and Glinda more or less presides over the South, where her castle is located. In *Land*, when General Jinjur prepares to conquer Oz with her all-girl army, the uniform selected consists of a green blouse, and a skirt with four panels representing the colors of the points of the compass.

The device is a not-so-pale echo of a much-quoted folk tale from Yorubaland, West Africa, about the trickster-divinity Edshu, who puts on a hat which is red on one side, white on the other, black behind, and green in the front (the colors of the four directions), in order to cause dissension among the people who see him. (Some say he wore a white hat, some red, depending upon what side he was viewed from.) One of the principal commentators upon this anecdote has been Joseph Campbell,[47] who sees Edshu as a personification of the Center, the axis mundi, or World Navel, a notion central to nearly all mythic systems. In Buddhism, of course, this axis occurs beneath the Bo Tree, or Tree of Enlightenment, and in Judaism at Sinai. The point is, however, that the center performs the syncretic function of joining the unlike in perfect harmony. In Oz the Emerald City is the axis and Ozma its personification.

No special logic can perhaps be made to attach to Baum's assignment of directional colors. In Navaho iconography, Campbell notes,[48] the colors are white, blue, yellow, and black. The rationale of this distribution makes white stand for the light of dawn in the

east, blue (south) for the daytime sky, yellow for evening light from the west, and black (north) for night.
Baum at least agrees that yellow is appropriate to the
west.

We have noted before the almost overwhelming
femaleness of Baum's fictional world, and this factor
becomes doubly important when examining this world
in the light of mythology. For the female presides quite
naturally over the infantile paradise, an area in which
the father can be nothing more than an intruder,
tolerated at best, regarded as an enemy at worst. But a
distinction should be made between this idea and the
inaccurate statement often made by critics that Baum's
is a "girls' world." Though apparently no popularity
survey has ever been made which would divide the loyal
Oz readership by sex, it seems safe to judge that he has
never lacked for male readers. There is a vast difference
between juvenile literature written *for* girls, and that
which utilizes the maternal and the virginal as ideals.
For the primal relationship to the mother is an experience peculiar to neither sex, and by extension the same
is true of the relationship of the human being to the
world. According to Campbell:

> The mythological figure of the Universal
> Mother imputes to the cosmos the feminine
> attributes of the first, nourishing and pro-
> tecting presence. The fantasy is primarily
> spontaneous; for there exists a close and
> obvious correspondence between the attitude
> of the young child toward its mother and
> that of the adult toward the surrounding
> material world. But there has been also, in
> numerous religious traditions, a consciously

controlled pedagogical utilization of this archetypal image for the purpose of purging,
balancing, and initiation of the mind into the
nature of the visible world.

In the Tantric books of medieval and modern
India the abode of the goddess is called mani-
dvipa, "The Island of Jewels." Her couch-
and-throne is there, in a grove of wish-fulfilling
trees. The beaches of the isle are of golden
sands. They are laved by the still waters of
the ocean of the nectar of immortality. The
goddess is red with the fire of life; the earth,
the solar system, the galaxies of far-extending
space, all swell within her womb. For she is
the world creatrix, ever mother, ever virgin.
She encompasses the encompassing, nourishes
the nourishing, and is the life of everything
that lives.[49]

Of the fourteen Oz books by Baum, four do have
male protagonists, although one of these (Tip in *Land*)
is, as we have seen, really a little girl bewitched, and
that little girl the ruling princess and ranking mother-
goddess figure. There is also the supportive mother-
figure in Glinda the Good of the Oz cycle, and another
in the regenerate Queen Zixi of Ix, out of the cycle.
But, true to the pattern outlined above, there are no
authoritative father-figures in all of Baum's work.

The Wizard is a self-confessed fraud, and one of the
masks he assumes in the early book is that of a beautiful
woman. After an escape by balloon from his failures in
Oz in this first story, he returns to the series reclaimed
from ignominy, but it is soon made clear that ". . .
Glinda has taught him all the real magic he knows, and

she is his superior in all sorts of sorcery." And though two other central figures, the Woodman and the Scarecrow, assume the role of adult male in the books, they are incapable of procreation by the necessity of their condition, if not the laws of Oz, so this diminishes considerably any sense of maleness or fatherhood they might otherwise convey.

Further, the condition of being female is exalted in exposition as well as example. During the early part of *Land*, Tip is only a passive agent of the powerful female, Mombi, his domineering foster mother. And in a late chapter, faced with the necessity of being transformed once more into a girl so he can ascend the throne of Oz, he feebly objects: "I don't want to be a girl!" But the Woodman tells him, "Never mind, old chap . . . it don't hurt to be a girl, I'm told; and we will all remain your faithful friends just the same. And, to be honest with you, I've always considered girls nicer than boys."[50] Nor is there ever another demur or regret from Tip-Ozma throughout the series.

The Nome King is male, but helpless against the most feminine of all symbols, the egg.

Females also appear regularly in roles which normal expectation would require to be filled by males. For instance, in *John Dough* the chief executioner (who is never permitted to execute anyone) is a girl, and in *The Patchwork Girl*, Tollydiggle, the turnkey at the Oz jail is, as we have seen, a motherly woman.

In *Yew* the hero, Prince Marvel, is really a female fairy temporarily transformed (just as Tip is in *Land*), who returns to his female form at the close of the story, and in the same book the dreaded High Ki, ruler of the land of Twi, where everything is double and the residents are of course called Twis, turns out to be twin girls, or more accurately, the id and ego of one girl. For the plot depends on an accident of magic which causes a schizoidal disaster: the two halves of this single person begin violently to disagree.

Dorothy's Uncle Henry is sickly, and plainly dominated by Aunt Em. Andy Omby, the private-turned-captain general, is superficially a seminal male, a character possibly derivative of Bluntschli in Shaw's *Arms and the Man*. But he remains a two-dimensional shadow, even when he joins the protagonal group of adventurers in *The Emerald City*. Similarly, Private Files (*Tik-Tok*) of Queen Ann Soforth's army evidently has sufficient libido to carry off the Rose Princess in the end, but both are also minor and poorly developed characters, not heard of outside the single book.

Another comment on female superiority is offered in *The Lost Princess* when Ugu tries to fend off his enemies with an illusory female army bearing "long pointed spears and sharp battle axes." The Frog Man says, "Girls are the fiercest soldiers of all. . . . They are more brave than men and they have better nerves. . . ."

Male assumption of the female persona, initiated with the Wizard, occurs again when the First and Foremost Phanfasm (*Emerald City*) ". . . slowly raised his arms, and in a twinkling his hairy skin fell from him and he appeared before the astonished Nome as a beautiful woman, clothed in a flowing gown of pink gauze. In her dark hair flowers were entwined, and her face was noble and calm." No females in Oz, however, voluntarily assume male identity. And out of Oz Prince Marvel (*Yew*) plans at the start to inhabit his male form for only a single year.

Moreover, unless they are semi-caricatures like

Aunt Em, or objects of fear like the witches, feminine characters do not fail to have extraordinary beauty, and usually virtue as well. Even Princess Langwidere (*Ozma*), though her virtue is in some doubt and not just because of her vanity—would she really have added Dorothy's head to her collection, and where did she get all those heads in the first place?—is attractively presented. Her thirty interchangeable heads are all splendidly coiffed, and she spends her days trying them on in a roomful of mirrors.

And in this fairyland where rule by the female is the norm, only one case is presented in which a male ruler is preferred, or even thought of. In *Tik-Tok* the newly picked Rose Princess is rejected by her disloyal subjects. ". . . we won't have her! We want a King! No girl shall rule over us."[51] The roses themselves seem to be all female, which might help explain the reluctance, along with the fact that the Rose Kingdom is outside Oz.

Unsurprisingly, there is no sexual congress in Oz, though there is an occasional pairing off of male and female characters. In *The Patchwork Girl* the Scarecrow, upon seeing Scraps for the first time, says:

> 'Forgive me for staring so rudely, but you are the most beautiful sight my eyes have ever beheld.'

> 'That is a high compliment from one who is himself so beautiful,' murmured Scraps, casting down her suspender-button eyes by lowering her head.[52]

This strange affair is pursued through the single book, but not beyond it.

Private Files and his Rose Princess have been mentioned, but they perhaps present more of a sexual problem than a case of true love. Though he is plainly enamored of her, he is carnal and she is presumably vegetable—or at least she started out that way. Their tepid attraction provides the opportunity for sexual symbolism, rare in Baum, when the Nome King turns the princess into a fiddle and threatens to turn Files into a bow. But it should be kept in mind that this story was Baum's single "adult" Oz book, written from the play-script. And the chances are in any case that he was less interested in suggestiveness than in the implied pun (bow-beau).

In the same book we encounter a suggestion of the rape of Persephone. When Polychrome the Rainbow's daughter, a sky fairy and a John Held Junior girl both in the text and in the Neill visualization, is proposed to by the Nome King, he says: ". . . I'll make a bargain with you, sweet Polly. Remain here and live with me and I'll set all these people free. You shall be my daughter or my wife or my aunt or grandmother—whichever you like—only stay here to brighten my gloomy kingdom and make me happy!"[53] Of course Polychrome, so obviously out of her element in the underground kingdom, assists in rescuing the prisoners in another way, and does not stay, even for part of a year.

For the most overt love story in Oz, however, we must go to *The Scarecrow* and the problem of Pon the Gardener's Boy and Princess Gloria, who face separation because of the traditional arranged marriage. The chosen fiancé for Gloria is predictably loathesome, and her father predictably adamant. But for some reason, intentional or not, instead of the young lover pitting

his strength and cleverness against his enemies to win
the princess, Pon comes on as a hysterical neurotic. His
sole contribution to the action is, in fact, a habit of
weeping and wailing over the imminent disaster. Even
sympathetic Betsy Bobbin thinks the Princess could do
better than Pon and says so, but Gloria instructs her:

> 'When you are older you will realize that a
> young lady cannot decide whom she will love,
> or choose the most worthy. Her heart alone
> decides for her, and whomsoever her heart
> selects, she must love, whether he amounts
> to much or not.[54]

Needless to add, when Pon acquires the princess
at last, it is through none of his own effort. Since
Baum is said to have regarded *The Scarecrow* as his
own favorite Oz book, perhaps he meant the tale of
Pon and Gloria to correct the stereotyped love story
found in traditional fairy tales by bringing it into some
kind of adjustment with "real" life. If so, the realism
falls short. Child readers looking to Baum for instruc-
tion in affairs of the heart are instead treated to a view
even more incredibly romantic than most. For if Gloria
believes what she tells Betsy, then Pon could have been
even more useless than he is and still come off all right.

But in case any doubt remains about female
mastery in Oz, we have only to return once more to the
talking hen Billina, who manages to transcend sex alto-
gether in performing the most remarkable feat of femin-
inity in the series. Billina appears first in *Ozma*
(1907), and it is made clear in that book that she is the
only chicken the Land of Oz has ever seen. She brings
no eggs with her from Kansas, and yet we discover four

books (and six years) later that she has hatched seven thousand chickens since coming to live in Oz.[55] This seems excessive even discounting the fact that none of her eggs could have been fertile. Back in Kansas a healthy brood hen in a normal year can hatch at most about ten clutches of some fourteen eggs each. Although the Shaggy Man plainly states, ". . . that's about seven thousand chicks she has hatched out . . ," it is just possible that he might be mistakenly attributing to Billina progeny really hatched by her daughters, grand-daughters, and so on. For we have already been in-formed (*Emerald City*) that nine of Billina's original family have survived to become "respectable hens," though "the other two turned out to be horrid roosters. . . ." Even so, this seems an unparalleled feat of parthenogenesis, one no doubt possible only in Oz.

Writers about Baum have occasionally speculated on the chances of Dorothy's being the literary incarna-tion of the daughter Baum never had in real life, and this would apply as well to all the other little-girl hero-ines including Ozma. As long as Oz is considered only as the wish-fulfillment device of its author, which of course it is, the point seems a likely, even an obvious one, especially since it is a biographical fact how Baum's hopes ran before each of his children was born. (She was to have been named Geraldine.)

But the overweening sentimentality about young females which infiltrates the later Oz books has its roots in far more than personal frustration, or even in fidelity to mythic expectations in such an eden as Oz. As a Victorian, Baum supported the code which had long since translated the normal male interest in deflowering maidens into a worship of virginity. Perpetuation of such a cult well past the turn of the century was only to be expected in a generation of males nurtured on Little Nell and Eva, Dorothy Vernon of Haddon Hall, *When Knighthood Was in Flower*, and *Pollyana, the Glad Girl*. Baum, functioning as high priest of this cult in America just as Lewis Carroll had done in England, accordingly chose for his heroines the extreme exemplar of the venerated category: girl children so young their purity could never be doubted. And placed them in Oz, where children do not grow, and the usual worldly progression from innocence to experience cannot apply.

Probably far more than is useful has already been written by psychologists, folklorists, and mythologists about the archetypal journey of the hero who, with or without magical assistance from the gods, leaves his society to undergo a series of trials which results in his death, symbolic or actual, after which he overcomes the obstacles for a symbolic or actual rebirth, and returns to his community bearing the secret of the gods which is to renew life among his kind. The remarkable thing about this formula in connection with Baum's work is that, using for the most part his little-girl "heroes," he was able to apply it very successfully in individual books, especially the early books. But when the idea was stretched to encompass the whole series, something was lost—as we shall see.

In the traditional fairy tale, some catastrophe, accident, or temporary failure of wit usually sets events in motion. A princess drops a ball she is playing with into a well, Childe Roland's sister thoughtlessly goes around a church widdershins and disappears, Jack stupidly allows himself to be done out of his property for a handful of beans. Baum faithfully complies, with his cyclone, earthquake, shipwreck, whirlpool, and John Dough's accident with the July Fourth rocket. And achieves the result that his protagonists and—more importantly—his readers are transported at once to the fairyland, the adventure begins immediately (in the case of John Dough the adventure actually begins before the transportation), and no interest is lost. By contrast C. S. Lewis's children in the first book take many pages to get to Narnia after several false starts, and McCutcheon uses up fully a third of his book just getting his hero to Graustark.

But to confine the examination to *The Wizard*, which offers by far the finest Baumian example of traditional management of the fairy tale, Dorothy, once over the first threshhold, receives the traditional magical assistance from the good witch, who implants the kiss of protection, and suggests Dorothy wear the shoes of the vanquished bad witch. The kiss and the shoes are the skein of thread Ariadne gives Theseus before he confronts the Minotaur in the labyrinth, the invincible bow Hercules (Herakles) presents to Philoctetes in the Greek legend of the wound and the bow. The trials of Dorothy scarcely need recapitulation. She does seek what in a traditional fairy tale or myth would be reconciliation with the father (Wizard). But since the latter turns out to be no great, helping father at all, her trials are multiplied. After finding him, she must go on a secondary journey at his behest, to demolish the second witch, and in the end, when she discovers that the resources she needs to achieve her goal had been hers all along, the story is seen to be an allegory of self-reliance, bolstered by the similar experiences of her companions, the Lion, Woodman, and Scarecrow. But it is nonetheless still in the tradition of the myth and fairy tale. For Dorothy's experience is almost identical to that of the Celtic superhero Cuchulainn, who undergoes many trials trying to

win the maiden Emer, but when he returns to find
the girl's father, Forgall the Wily, still against him,
Cuchulainn simply carries Emer off, for "the adventure
itself had given him the capacity to annihilate all
opposition."[56]

Another superb Baum plot deserving of special
treatment here is that of *John Dough*, which from a
mythic standpoint becomes a tour de force of a burlesque on the flight of the hero from the wrath of the
gods after the theft of the secret of immortality, or the
elixir of imperishable being, or the fire of life. Sometimes the hero is caught and punished (as Prometheus),
and sometimes he gets home free (Jason with the fleece),
but whatever the outcome the tale is so central to so
many cultures that the reiterations are seemingly inex-
haustible. To begin early, Gilgamesh, the Sumerian
hero, sets out on a quest for the watercress of immortality, the plant called "Never Grow Old." After many
vicissitudes, he dives into the depths of the cosmic sea
and brings up the magic plant, only to lose it on the way
home when he stops to rest and a serpent runs off with
it. In the Hindu account of the primordial battle
between the titans and the gods, the titan high priest
gains the favor of Shiva, who gives him the elixir. But
the gods enlist the help of Brahma and Vishnu, who
advise churning the Milky Ocean of immortal life for
its "butter," *amrita*, the "nectar of deathlessness." The
gods end up with the *amrita*, and after another battle
in which the titans are defeated, retire to dine upon it
forever. And there is the Welsh folk tale of Gwion
Bach, who visits the Land Under Waves where Caridwen
stirs a black mixture in an open kettle over a fire.
After a year, the cauldron is to produce three precious
drops: the grace of inspiration. Gwion is charged by

Caridwen with stirring the pot, but toward the end of the year, three drops fly out of the mess and land on his finger. He automatically puts his finger to his mouth to ease the burning, and consumes the elixir. A thundering pursuit follows.[57]

In *John Dough* the Arab assumes the role of the god from whom the elixir is stolen, and the theft is inadvertent when Mme. Leontyne mixes up the bottles entrusted to her care, and pours the elixir into a basin of water to soak her rheumatic limbs. Her husband, uninformed about the matter, rises early to make a gingerbread man in his bakeshop; the dough needs moisture, and he adds the water from the basin. John Dough comes to life, the Arab perceives what has happened and pursues him, as do others who hear of the adventure and also want to eat bits of the gingerbread and so gain immortal life. John achieves the apotheosis fitting a true elixir hero when he becomes king of Hiland and Loland.

Nor does Baum discard the elixir theme after this story, but weaves it into the very fabric of Oz. The Sawhorse and Jack Pumpkinhead (*Land*) owe their mobility if not existence to the Powder of Life. So does the Gump. The plot of *The Patchwork Girl* depends upon a variation of the motif when Dr. Pipt, the Crooked Magician, manufactures the Powder (stirring a cauldron for a year or so in the manner of the Welsh goddess Caridwen) in order to bring to life his wife Margolotte's life-sized patchwork doll, and make her the family servant. (He has already worked the experiment successfully on a glass cat.) But during a visit from Ojo and his Unc Nunkie, the accident of the two flasks introduced in *John Dough* is repeated. The Powder brings the Patchwork Girl to life all right, and also a Victrola which receives an inadvertent sprinkling, but in the confusion the bottle containing the Liquid of Petrifaction is spilled on Ojo's uncle and the magician's wife. The ensuing quest by Ojo to acquire the ingredients for a new batch of elixir (powder) is thwarted but Ozma intervenes and restores the two victims of petrifaction to life by magic. This outcome is satisfactory because Ozma's is a legal magic, while Dr. Pipt's was not.

The antithesis of the elixir, the rendering of characters immobile or inanimate as in the story of Lot's Wife, had already been exploited by Baum in *Ozma* when the Nome King, after having turned the royal family of Ev into trinkets for his underground palace, proceeds to do the same to the visitors from Oz. And in later stories Ozma is transformed into a peach pit (*Lost Princess*) while elsewhere Trot and Cap'n Bill are magically turned into shrub-like beings with roots growing deep in the ground, which suggests rather the story of the nymph Daphne, turned into a laurel tree by her river-god father Peneus, while she was being pursued by Apollo. But in these latter instances, the device is only incidental to the plot.

A related mythic motif, and one also (like the elixir) integral with the concept of Oz as the garden of paradise, is also developed with some imagination—as well as borrowings from tradition—as Baum proceeds through his series. In the first book food grows abundantly on the land and overnight accommodations are available at the farm homes of Ozites. Dorothy lives on nuts and fruit after her bread and cheese from Kansas run out.

Refinements in later books include trees which bear box lunches and dinner pails (*Ozma*), "three-course nuts" which are slightly larger than coconuts and con-

tain hot soup, an entree, and dessert (*Tik-Tok*), and—
in the same book—a full description of life in Oogaboo
where all necessary things grow in orchards tended by
citizens named for the crops they raise. Thus when Ann
conscripts her army, her officers are named Apple, Bun,
Cone, Clock, Plum, Egg, Banjo, Cheese and so on.
Private Files, unsurprisingly, grows files in his orchard,
but he also grows books, "which are picked and husked
and ready to read. If they were picked too soon, the
stories were found to be confused and uninteresting,
and the spelling bad. However, if allowed to ripen
perfectly, the stories were fine reading and the spelling
and grammar excellent." And in *The Tin Woodman*
we discover the redoubtable General Jinjur has retired
to a farm, where she raises fields of cream puffs,
chocolate-caramels, and macaroons.

In view of this, it is difficult to imagine that Baum
was unfamiliar with Jainist teachings. For in the past
golden age of this Hindu sect (or rather in one of the
several golden ages) there were ten "wish-fulfilling trees"
(*kalpa vriksha*), "and on these grew sweet fruits, leaves
that were shaped like pots and pans, leaves that sweetly
sang, leaves that gave forth light at night, flowers delightful to see and to smell, food perfect both to sight and
to taste, leaves that might serve as jewelry, and bark
providing beautiful clothes. One of the trees was like
a many-storied palace in which to live; another shed a
gentle radiance, like that of many little lamps. The earth
was sweet as sugar; the ocean as delicious as wine."[58]
The device reminds us as well of the Valley of Mo
(*supra*, p. 57).

And just as food in Oz ranges from the simple to
the complex, so do the overnight accommodations.
After the first book where Dorothy spends the night

with a Munchkin farm family, cottages with waiting beds and warm suppers begin to be provided magically, or whole campsites elaborately described materialize in the same manner, as when the Wizard produces tents for all out of pocket handkerchiefs in *The Emerald City*. Though later wanderers in Oz do occasionally rest in more natural surroundings, on beds of soft leaves under the stars, this is not the rule but the exception.

One service missing from Oz is transportation, at least in the early books. One can walk across the land, border to border, in several days, passing through meadows and groves, fording an occasional stream. And this is important to plot, for some of the obstacles to be tackled by the protagonal group are part of the landscape, like the fighting trees, the whirling merry-go-round mountains, the disappearing city, the illusory barriers already discussed, a river that flows first one direction and then in the opposite direction, and many more. When rides are provided in the early stories, they are products of a combination of inventiveness and magic, such as the Saw Horse Tip brings to life for the sole purpose of serving Jack Pumpkinhead as a mount, or the flying Gump which he fashions out of a pair of sofas and other unlikely paraphernalia from the royal palace. Ozma later uses the Saw Horse to pull the royal conveyances on visits to outlying parts of her kingdom. But the atmosphere of slow journeying, surrounded by repletion, with no thought of wealth-seeking because there is no need, and no thought for the morrow for all will be provided, is never quite lost entirely, even toward the end of the series.

One part of this last sentence, however, should be enlarged upon. For while it is true there is no acquisitiveness among the "good" Ozites, a number of the pro-

tagonal characters do make rather spectacular, rags-to-
riches ascents. Moreover, most of these take the form
of commoner-promoted-to-monarch, in the best Cinder-
ella tradition. The Woodman becomes Emperor of the
Winkies; the Scarecrow becomes ruler of Oz upon the
defection of the Wizard; Tip becomes Ozma; John
Dough becomes king of Hiland and Loland, while the
Cherub, his beloved companion, becomes "head booley-
wag," or prime minister; Dorothy herself, for her many
services to the Ozites, is made a royal princess of Oz.
Even that doubtful hero Pon the Gardener's Boy becomes consort to Queen Gloria. Most dramatic of all is
the crowning of King Bud, who, as we have noted,
achieves royalty by surprise and entirely by chance.

Only Nikobob[59] the charcoal burner, a minor
character in *Rinkitink*, declines leadership of his people
when it is offered, explaining:

> I have noticed that some men become rich,
> and are scorned by some and robbed by
> others. Other men become famous and are
> mocked at and derided by their fellows. But
> the poor and humble man who lives unnoticed
> and unknown escapes all these troubles and is
> the only one who can appreciate the joy of
> living.[60]

These rises to royal status no doubt reflect the
up-from-nothing spirit of the author's time as well as
adherence to the rule of romantic literature which
requires the upward movement plus attention to the
lives of kings and princesses. Nor do we want to leave
out of account Baum's own long striving to be a prince
among princes—especially in the theater, and if not

there, *some*where.   After all, Baum's title "Royal Historian of Oz" was self-bestowed.

But the rise to the throne is not the only strange trend in the touted classless society of Oz. (Classless, that is, for all except the monarch herself and her court, for it is understood that here is a monarchy.) It turns out that for all Baum's protestations of the value of the individual, in Oz some individuals are more valuable than others.   In *Dorothy and the Wizard* Ozma is particularly happy to receive Dorothy in Oz because "girls of [Ozma's] own age with whom it was proper for the Princess to associate were very few. . . ." And in *Rinkitink* the Tottenhots, who are apparently dark-skinned, with negroid hair, are described as "a lower form of a man."

On the other hand, the story of Scraps is evidently an implied lesson in equality.   Scraps is created for the sole purpose of serving as maid-of-all-work.   Dame Margolotte says, "I must be careful not to give her too much brains, and those she has must be such as are fitted to the station she is to occupy in life. In other words, her brains mustn't be very good . . . a servant with too much brains is sure to become independent and high-and-mighty and feel above her work."[61]   But when Scraps is brought to life, she has no feeling of inferiority, no "proper" servile mentality, quite the contrary, for Ojo has mischievously added more of the magical brain ingredients while Margolotte's back was turned.   Nor has Scraps the faintest intention of living in a condition of slavery in a remote backwater of Oz. She goes to the Emerald City to make a life of her own, and remains there as a guest of Ozma and favorite of Dorothy.   Margolotte, meanwhile, is accidentally turned to stone as an indirect, if not direct, result of her folly.

In sifting through the material of Oz in order to discover in what ways Baum departs from the traditional image of the golden age, it would almost seem from his emphasis on the natural, pastoral setting that he has closer kinship with the William Morris who created the medieval-pastoral "Nowhere" than with such writers as Edward Bellamy, who gave their attention to projected technical wonderlands of the future. Yet that conclusion is not quite accurate. It can *almost* be said that Baum, born to an age of empiricism, employed the powers of his adult period of productivity to escape via his own fiction into the realm of the metaphysical. But not quite. For such an assessment does not take into consideration how very much a product of his own era the author was, and further neglects the fictional lengths to which Baum took his natural enthusiasm for the mechanical gadget, which, to the layman of the time, appeared to be the end product of science. Baum accordingly took gadgetry along with him to the Land of Oz (even as the youthful counterculture of today uses the electronic amplifier and the stroboscopic light, while rejecting out of hand the "plastic" technology which produced them).

For the first time in the history of the fairy tale, Baum produces monsters which are mechanical, in whole or part, like the Wheelers (*Ozma*), whose arms and legs end in casters instead of hands and feet. Or the one-wheeled automobile on the Isle of Phreex (*John Dough*), which relentlessly flattens all in its path and makes of Baum a minor prophet of the freeway culture. Even dragons are modified; the most memorable is Quox (*Tik-Tok*), who is a traditional dragon in every way, except that the tip of his tail is a perennially lit Edison electric globe. The Ork is another case in point.

Ostensibly a bird, it has a mechanical tail which spins like a boat propeller to aid the animal in aerial—and occasional aquatic—locomotion, a kind of amphibious helicopter which has yet to be invented.

But undoubtedly the most significant result of this shotgun wedding of the machine age to medieval magic is that Baum pioneered a gimmick which has since become a convention of twentieth-century fantasy: the robot. Baum did not use the word; that came later with Karel Capek, who is credited with coining the term from the Russian word "robotchny," which means "worker."[62]   In pre-Baumian literature the robot had been approached but never achieved. Mary Shelley's creation, though factitious, was not mechanical, nor was the Golem of Prague. Not until Tik-Tok, Baum's clockwork man, appears is a genuine robot to be found in imaginative literature.

That is, unless one counts the cast-iron man in Baum's own *Magical Monarch of Mo*, 1900. The iron creature is a machine made for the sole purpose of marching across the Valley of Mo, crushing trees and houses. Since he is capable only of this one act, the people of Mo solve their dilemma simply by pointing him about-face, in the direction of the enemy who sent him, and letting the iron monster have a go at the enemy's trees and houses. And in the same book which introduces Tik-Tok to the series (*Ozma*), a similar giant mechanical man, programmed to one job only, pounding the path to the entrance of the underground world of the Nomes—he performs precisely the function of the Symplegades in Greek mythology—appears to terrorize would-be visitors there. But while these iron men can properly be considered robots, neither is of course as fully realized as Tik-Tok, who walks, talks, and thinks, *if* his friends remember to wind up the appropriate keys.

A faint foreshadowing of Tik-Tok also occurs in *Father Goose*:

> Now, once I owned a funny man,
> A Clock-work was inside him;
> You'd be surprised how fast he ran
> When I was there beside him.
> He was the pride of all the boys
> Who lived within our town;
> But when this man ran up a hill
> He always would run down!

The difference is that Tik-Tok is not a toy. Like the Woodman, he is man-sized, but unlike the Woodman, he is not alive, which is why he is a true robot and the Woodman is not. Furthermore, it is made clear that Tik-Tok has no emotions, as none were built into him by his creators, Smith and Tinker. But the Oz crowd graciously accepts him, all the same, as one of themselves.

Technology again came to Baum's aid after that great crisis in which Oz was cut off from all contact with the real world. A note to the author from "Dorothy Gale" appeared in *The Emerald City* in a final chapter entitled "How the Story of Oz Came to an End." It warned Baum and his readers that "You will never hear anything more about Oz, because we are now cut off forever from all the rest of the world. . . ." According to Daniel P. Mannix, the maneuver caused an uproar comparable to the panic in London after A. Conan Doyle threw Holmes off a cliff.[63] Acceding to popular demand two years later, Baum re-established contact by wireless. Marconi's invention was the newest thing on the technological front at the time.

Perhaps Baum's most ambitious merger of magic and engineering occurs in *Glinda*, where a vast basement power plant raises and lowers an entire glass-domed island in the center of a lake. Judging by the author's somewhat detailed explanation, the thing works like an automobile hoist, the island resting on a vertical steel beam. As an embellishment to the "invention," it is possible to leave the island when it is submerged via an automatic submarine which emerges from a power-operated door in the wall of the basement room. The rub comes when we learn that the machinery for the hoist and sub can be operated only by pronouncing a magic word, and the only sorceress who knows the word has been turned into a swan (voiceless). Glinda, the good sorceress, comes to the rescue of the protagonists, who are trapped, of course, in the island dome when it is submerged. An important part of Glinda's rescue equipment is a "skeropythrope," apparently some kind of lantern or crucible on a tripod, the gadget designed to emit sparks when magic ingredients are dusted over its surface. Thus a device appropriate to alchemy triumphs in the end over twentieth-century mechanization.

During this same episode, Baum makes one of his numerous references to radium. The Wizard, who is assisting Glinda, says of an unknown magic powder, "It may be some kind of radium." But Glinda replies, "No, it is more wonderful than even radium. . . ." Earlier, in *The Patchwork Girl*, the Horners are discovered to be using radium for interior decorating, and because it is so much in demand—it is credited with medicinal qualities as well as decorative—operate a radium mine in order to produce it in quantity. What Baum thought radium was is conjectural. It should not be forgotten,

however, that the metal had been first isolated by the
Curies as recently as 1898, and that a little radio-
activity certainly couldn't have harmed the immortal
Ozites anyhow.

One of the preliminary conclusions which seems
to emerge from this account of Baum's highly eclectic
eden, as it appears in his fairylands in and out of Oz, is
that he probably stumbled onto the archetypal formula
after trial and error (and emulation of other writers),
and manipulated its elements more or less intuitively.
If he occasionally and selfconsciously injects material
which is inappropriate, or which does not "work" in the
setting chosen, almost as often he falls back on a rich
repository of the unconscious through which he is able
to reach heights and plumb depths probably not otherwise accesible to him.

Some of his experimentation is painfully apparent
in early work. By all accounts, Baum originally saw no
more merit in Oz than in his other stories. And in this
he was quite right insofar as *John Dough* and *Queen
Zixi* are concerned, and to a lesser extent *Yew* and
possibly *Mo*. But in 1901, a year after *The Wizard*
came out, but before anyone could have predicted the
real extent of its popularity, a Baum work called *American Fairy Tales* appeared. Russel B. Nye quite justi-
fiably comments on this book (which may or may not
have been written after the first Oz story) by complain-
ing that the author

 . . . failed to observe the first rule of the
 wonder-tale—that it must create a never-never
 land in which all laws of probability may be
 credibly contravened or suspended. . . .
 Baum nevertheless clung for a few years to

the belief that he could make the United
States an authentic fairyland. 'There's lots of
magic in all nature,' he remarked in *Tik-Tok
of Oz*, 'and you may see it as well in the
United States, where you and I once lived, as
you can here.' But children could not. They
saw magic only in Oz, which never was nor
could be Chicago or Omaha or California or
Kansas.[64]

This experience, of having readers regard fairy tales
set in America as inferior to those laid in Oz, apparently
warned Baum not to mix the norms of his locations,
though he compromised—and gained conviction—by
continuing to begin most of his tales in the United
States, but with a difference. The magic shoes Dorothy
acquires in the first book are lost in the Deadly Desert;
later (*Ozma*) she is careful to leave the Nome King's
belt with Ozma, knowing its powers of enchantment
won't work in Kansas; the pet hen does not speak until
Dorothy washes ashore in the Land of Ev, one of those
areas adjacent to the desert surrounding Oz, and hence
a fairyland. And though she has the magic to command
their services, Dorothy cannot insist that the Winged
Monkeys (*The Wizard*) carry her back to Kansas for the
very good reason that

'We belong to this country alone, and cannot
leave it. There has never been a Winged Mon-
key in Kansas yet, and I suppose there never
will be, for they don't belong there.'[65]

In a Borderland of Oz story (a label shrewdly
coined by Baum's publisher in an attempt to deflect

some of the popularity of Oz to the other fairy tales), the old sea captain and Trot (*Sea Fairies*) do encounter mermaids on the California off-shore, perhaps beyond the territorial limits, perhaps not. Another exception occurs in *John Dough* when the Elixir brings the gingerbread man to life in America as magically as the Powder of Life does Jack Pumpkinhead in Oz. But then the Elixir is the property of the Arab, and was brought from the incomprehensible Orient, practically a fairyland itself in down-to-earth Yankee thinking.

In general, then, in Baum's best work, either the magic is restricted to the exotic locale or, if it occurs in a non-fairyland, it made strikingly appropriate to its location. Dorothy might well fall into a cleavage in the earth during a quake if she were in California early in the century. So with the funnel-shaped windstorm on the Great Plains. Furthermore, it is plausible that Dorothy's house should be picked up and whirled away—half a mile or a thousand, what's the difference? Even adults can willingly accept the initial premise; children will not balk at the next, that the house comes down on a wicked witch. For the second premise is appropriate to the new locale, if not the old.

In the classic fairy tale, into which category several of Baum's non-Oz books fall, *Queen Zixi* in particular, the reader is not presented with this step-by-step chance to accept the improbable; the whole mythos is revealed immediately: take it or leave it. In the Oz series, on the other hand, Baum tested and found valid the rule that latter-day fantasy depends far more than other genres upon Coleridge's "willing suspension of disbelief." In most cases its plausibility (and acceptability) depends upon this same acceptance of an initial hypothesis not repugnant to credulity, which may or may not proceed to another more or less acceptable hypothesis. Just as in Oz, the reader is never given the chance to exclaim, with Alice, "Why you're only a pack of cards!"

It seems very likely, in fact, that in any ultimate assessment of Baum's books for children, his greatest strength and the source of his endurance will be seen to stem from the fundamental appeal of his mythic themes, combined with this imaginatively maintained high degree of conviction.

Beside these qualities even his other virtues seem overshadowed, though they should not be ignored. He was indeed wonderfully inventive. Like Lewis Carroll he understood how to write for young people without "talking down." Though he was never guilty of the kind of auctorial moralizing which characterizes the Charles Kingsley school of children's literature, his work does offer guidance painlessly stated and demonstrated which is at best useful and at worst inoffensive. And he could hold the attention of adults while speaking more directly to younger readers, as we have seen.

Not to be neglected either is the fact that Baum stories move briskly, and while there are occasional Pickwickian pauses for the story-within-the-story, the insertions are always as action-filled as the mainline adventure.

Baum is occasionally congratulated as well upon his clarity, and for the most part it is true that his language constructions are straightforward and that he avoids the alien expression and the polysyllabic word. This makes the more remarkable his occasional use of a word such as "retroussé."[66]

But there is a misapprehension about Baum which deserves mention if only because it has been several times repeated. He is said by some to have ". . . possessed a flawless command of English,"[67] while in actuality, as any close reader of Baum knows, he was a master of the dangling modifier who also excelled at the frequent redundancy and the occasional solecism, hazards which could all have been avoided, incidentally, had he only been blessed with responsible copy editors.

Beginning with *The Wizard*, in which the travelers approach the city gate ("After ringing several times it was opened by the same Guardian of the Gates they had met before."), and proceeding through *The Road*, in which the Wizard blows a magical soap bubble around the Queen of Merryland ("When completed he allowed the bubble to float slowly upward . . ."), one may see that Baum's grasp of the function of the modifier did not improve with time. In *The Sea Fairies*, a middle book (1911), there is a description of Queen Aquareine and her party in conversation ("While thus engaged the gong at the door sounded and Sacho entered."), and in *Glinda*, the book Baum wrote quite literally on his deathbed, Ozma speaks as ungrammatically as ever a character did (". . . being princess of this fairyland it is my duty to make all my people . . . happy").

Meanwhile, the skies of Oz are never blue, but always blue *in color*. A character created by Baum may never be simply tall and thin; he is tall and thin *in appearance*. Less frequently, but quite as insistently, appear sentences such as ". . . then he [the Scarecrow] laid down and permitted them to pull the straw from his body."

As for spelling lapses, Baum was so consistently wrong about certain favorite words ("murmer" for "murmur" and "nickle" for "nickel") that the failures lend him a distinctively endearing quality. Surely "chipmonk" is as readily understandable as "chipmunk" and "colender" as "colander." The same for "accordeon." And although "pruning" and "preening" may claim an archaic synonymity, the numerous reports of birds "pruning" their feathers call up curious pictures, even considering these are Ozian birds. (He never learned how to spell "accomodate" either.)

Baum explained that his spelling change of "gnome" to "nome" was made to avoid confusion for the child readers. The same explanation apparently can be extended to cover an episode in *John Dough* wherein a composer shouts, "I am greater than Vogner." At the same time it is a question how many children have grown up with spelling problems on these words (and others), problems directly traceable to Baum.

But these are all minuscule, forgivable faults at worst. There remains to be mentioned a major flaw in flawless Oz, one that can be viewed both as a conscious, workaday problem of a series writer, and as an inherent failure of the golden-age archetype itself.

One of the primary objections of children's librarians and critics to series books in general is that while the original stories may be acceptable, the succeeding ones utilizing the same characters and settings tend to depend less on literary merit than on wilder, and consequently "thinner," variations on a single tested theme. Thus the child reader, for whom every book should open a new world and so extend his experience, is led time and again over the same known ground which annually grows more barren as the writer's imaginative faculty declines.

Baum is certainly not immune to this charge. The real difference between him and other series writers for children seems to be one of degree. For he managed to produce more than the usual number of creditable stories before the supply of creativity began to run low. The point is that it did run low.

The confusion connected with trying to establish exactly the point at which the Oz series begins to pall is brought about at least in part by the fact that the ingredients which made Baum's mixtures palatable ran out at different rates.

One of the first to go is the strong, no-nonsense character of Dorothy, Baum's first heroine and perhaps his best. Dorothy is, by virtue of her very presence in fairyland, innocent. And Dorothy's innocence is, as we have seen, never in jeopardy because in Oz there is no lapse between illusion and reality. As is proper to romantic literature, in which innocence is the traditional primary organizing idea, the two states are one in Oz.

Almost contradictorily, however, though Dorothy's "kindly and innocent heart" is offered by the author from time to time as a sort of recommendation to her role as heroine, it is actually her characterization as a child who employs courage, ingenuity, and Yankee common sense in facing reality which gives substance and charm to the early books in which she appears. She has a marked measure of maturity, is well able to assess situations accurately, make judgments, and act on those judgments, with no backwash of regret or remorse, or even of second thought.

Introduced as a Kansas farm child whose home, with herself and her dog inside, is blown by the storm into the Land of Oz, she does not panic during the hours the cabin is being buffeted along at the top of the updraft; when her dog accidentally falls through the open trapdoor which has once led to the storm cellar, she calmly fetches him back in (the updraft has kept him within reach, making the incident more or less anticipate the "space walk" of a later era), and secures the door before sensibly taking a nap in her own bed to wait out the excitement.

To the Wizard's thundering "I am Oz the Great and Terrible . . ," she firmly replies, "I am Dorothy, the Small and Meek . . ," but she is not really meek any more than the Wizard is really terrible. Faced with getting back home to Kansas, she sets about it with implacable determination. And when the Wizard makes it a condition of his helping her that she destroy the second witch, she sets out immediately to do it, even though she does not want to destroy anyone or anything.

It is in a struggle over Dorothy's magic shoes, of which the wicked sorceress knows the worth while Dorothy does not (for purposes of the allegory, Dorothy even yet does not apprehend the full power of her own inner resources), that water is spilled over the girl's enemy, who is at the time also her captress. The witch promptly melts away "like brown sugar before her very eyes."

But practical, self-reliant Dorothy is not one to waste time in pointless hysteria.

> . . . the Witch fell down in a brown, melted, shapeless mass and began to spread over the clean boards of the kitchen floor. Seeing that she had really melted away to nothing, Dorothy drew another bucket of water and threw it over the mess. She then swept it all out the door. After picking out the silver shoe, which was all that was left of the old woman, she cleaned and dried it with a cloth, and put it on her foot again. Then, being at

last free to do as she chose, she ran out to
the court-yard to tell the Lion that the
Wicked Witch of the West had come to an
end, and that they were no longer prisoners
in a strange land.[68]

Even failing all else, there is an object lesson in
tidiness here for the children.

That Baum never intended Dorothy's stardom in
more than the single book is obvious from the fact that,
even when he was faced with having to construct a
second Oz story, he chose to leave her out. *Land* has
no characters at all from "outside." Afterward, however, when demands were made by readers that Dorothy
re-appear, he was able to bring her back as much the
same self-sufficient little girl in *Ozma, Dorothy and the
Wizard*, and *Road*.

In the first of these, when the Oz party arrives at
the gates of the underground kingdom and the others
refuse to stoop to begging the Nome King to come out,
on grounds the act would lessen their dignity, Dorothy
volunteers; it will not lessen hers because "I'm only a
little girl from Kansas, and we've got more dignity at
home than we know what to do with. . . . I'll call the
Nome King."

But even in this book the corrosion is already at
work which will lead to the general disintegration not
only of Dorothy's character and personality, but those
of the other little-girl heroines. For Dorothy, from
Ozma on, becomes increasingly "cute," even coy, a
change evidenced most strikingly by the change in her
speech habits. Her syllables suddenly begin telescoping
("s'pose," "s'prise") and she almost inevitably begins
clauses with "'cause," in the manner of A. A. Milne

characters. It is a habit unthinkable in the plain-spoken Dorothy of the early days. *Her* diction was faultless.

"Send me back to Kansas, where my Aunt Em and Uncle Henry are," the "old" Dorothy pleads with the Wizard. ". . . I don't like your country, although it is so beautiful. And I am sure Aunt Em will be dreadfully worried over my being away so long." And when the Wizard asks why he should do this for her, she replies: "Because you are strong and I am weak; because you are a Great Wizard and I am only a helpless little girl."

In *Ozma* we first meet the "new" Dorothy, who tells Billina, while the hen is eating bugs: "You ought to be 'shamed of yourself! . . . I can't just 'splain the diff'rence. . . ." By *The Emerald City* apostrophes are spread thick enough to match any Joel Chandler Harris story, with "'cause," and ". . . she 'vised us . . ," and "I don't know, 'zactly." Since Dorothy, Betsy, Trot, and Cap'n Bill all take on the same habits of speech, and all—or most—of them appear together on some occasions, the minor problem becomes a major one as the plague spreads.

As Dorothy and the others become more coy, so do they become skittish and downright irritable, the kind of girls who shy at the sight of spiders. In *Magic*, when the Wizard is suddenly transformed into a fox, Dorothy exclaims: "Mercy me!" She has strayed a long mile now from the Dorothy who swept the melted witch out the door. This particular expletive, in fact, indicative of an accompanying excursion into phony-genteelism, comes into frequent use by the others too, including the Wizard himself, who shares in the pale-ing, deteriorating process.

Less objectionable, certainly, but symptomatic of

the same "decadent" trend are the spellings of girls'
names which appear in the later books. "Mayre," in
The Sea Fairies, for instance, and "Salye" in *Tik-Tok*.

Somehow, perhaps because Ozma originates in
fairyland and not in some quaint, outlandish place like
Kansas (Dorothy), or Oklahoma (Betsy), or California
(Trot), Ozma alone among the girl characters remains
unaffected by the epidemic of cuteness, and even of the
careless speech. *Her* degeneration is brought about,
however, in an even more painful way, as the descriptions take on a note of cloying, self-conscious sentimentality. The first description (*Land*) borders on the
effusive, but is sheer objectivity compared with that to
come:

> . . . a young girl, fresh and beautiful as a May
> morning. Her eyes sparkled as [sic] two
> diamonds, and her lips were tinted like a
> tourmaline. All adown her back floated
> tresses of ruddy gold, with a slender jeweled
> circlet confining them at the brow. Her robes
> of silken gauze floated around her like a
> cloud, and dainty satin slippers shod her
> feet.[69]

In the ninth book (*Scarecrow*), Baum has found a
few more stops to pull:

> As for Ozma herself, there are no words in
> any dictionary I can find that are fitted to
> describe this young girl's beauty of mind and
> person. Merely to see her is to love her for
> her charming face and manners; to know her
> is to love her for her tender sympathy, her

generous nature, her truth and honor. . . .
Born of a long line of Fairy Queens, Ozma
is as nearly perfect as any fairy may be and
she is noted for her wisdom as well as her
other qualities.[70]

There might have been comfort for Baum in
knowing—if he did—that at his worst he was reminiscent
of Dickens at *his* worst. For there is surely something
in Ozma as we find her in the thirteenth and penultimate
book (*Magic*) of Esther Summerson of *Bleak House* as
Esther proceeds with sunny cheer along the path of
duty, a sincere friend to even the most lowly, and so on.

She [Ozma] lived in the most magnificent
palace in the most magnificent city in the
world, but that did not prevent her from
being the friend of the most humble person
in her dominions . . . she would stop in a
forest to speak to a charcoal burner and ask
if he was happy . . . giving to each and all a
cheering word or sunny smile.[71]

But if Ozma and the other little girls tend to fade
into sentimental stereotypes, so do some of the new
characters, especially those introduced after *Road*, tend
to be less original and fully realized than their earlier
counterparts. Among those who never quite rise to the
stature of the Woodman, the Scarecrow, and the early
Cowardly Lion are Polychrome, who seems to be the
precise fictional equivalent of the calendar-art model so
often sketched by illustrator Neill, the Hungry Tiger,
and the Frog Man. The Shaggy Man, another later
arrival, is an exception, perhaps because he compels the

reader to give him all the attention and respect due the classic mysterious itinerant in fiction, the Wandering Jew with the Pearl of Great Price (Love Magnet) concealed in his tattered costume. And yet even here there is the feeling Shaggy has been dragged by main force to three-dimensional status; that is, he does make it, but Baum expends more visible effort on rendering him convincing, and this applies equally to Trot and Cap'n Bill. The Patchwork Girl, on the other hand, although she appears in a later book, manages to transcend this criticism; she is in fact endowed with some of the genuine good cheer and sensible judgment of the early Dorothy.

Among the lesser characters and inventions a similar differentiation is possible. The Gump's acceptability (*Land*) is due to its homeliness. It is exactly the kind of thing that would have been improvised by a boy like Tip, using handy paraphernalia and childishly inspired imagination. The flying machine in *John Dough*, though it is fetchingly bird-shaped, is "scientific," its principles and parts never discussed. Thus for the child reader, who has "helped" Tip assemble the Gump from items taken from the palace parlor, the suspension of disbelief is more joyful because it springs from deeper involvement.

But there are yet more of the ingredients that "ran out" in the series. The strange excesses to which the motif of everlasting life was put by Baum after he introduced it in the early stories have already been discussed in part. But the purpose it serves in *The Tin Woodman*, a late book, definitely shows this device, too, in serious decline. Nick Chopper, the Woodman's name during his former, flesh-and-blood life, meets by chance with another all-tin man, Captain Fyter, whose history is identical to Chopper's. Whereas the Woodman's series of accidents has been due to the enchantment placed on him by a witch trying to prevent his marriage to a Munchkin maiden, Fyter has received identical treatment from the same witch (except he has a sword instead of an ax) because of his attention to the same maiden. Since the two suitors have employed the same tinsmith, Ku-Klip, to fashion their new parts, the chopped-off flesh of both men has wound up in Ku-Klip's shop, which is in Oz, where nothing dies.

Chopper and Fyter decide to return to Nimee Aimee, the maiden who has now been abandoned by them both, so that she can choose between them. They locate her after many adventures, but to no purpose, since she is now happily wed to a man of flesh named Chopfyt, who turns out to be still another triumph of the tinsmith. Ku-Klip has fashioned him out of the cast-off parts of the now-tin men. The story not only provides a highly disturbing episode in the smith's shop in which Chopper has a dialogue with his own former head, but leaves the child reader with a very practical question: why didn't the tinsmith attach the living parts back where they belonged after they were first chopped off? Or, if he did not have the secret of the magic glue at that time—it was obtained later from the witch—he could at least have assembled the parts in their original order. Yet in any case there seems no way to relieve the oppressiveness, even gruesomeness, of the story.

Also reaching the saturation point along the way in the series was Baum's exploitation of the "strange race" for purposes of satire. Perhaps the device dies of overexposure in The Emerald City, for it is in this story that the peak is reached. Oz, it is understood, isolates

into separate colonies the types of people most likely
to make the lives of others difficult. The Fuddles constantly "go all to pieces" over nothing, and are conceived by Baum as three-dimensional jigsaw-puzzle people. The rambling conversation of the Rigmaroles,
already mentioned, mystifies Dorothy.

> 'It is the easiest thing in the world for a person
> to say "yes" or "no" when a question that is
> asked for the purpose of gaining information
> or satisfying the curiosity of the one who has
> given expression to the inquiry has attracted
> the attention of an individual who may be
> competent either from personal experience or
> the experience of others to answer it with
> more or less correctness or at least an attempt
> to satisfy the desire for information on the
> part of the one who has made the inquiry
> by—'
> 'Dear me!' exclaimed Dorothy, interrupting
> the speech. 'I've lost all track of what you
> were saying.'[72]

In the same book are the Whimsies, who have fitted
huge false heads over their own naturally small heads.
"They foolishly imagined that no one would suspect
the little heads that were inside the imitation ones, not
knowing that it is folly to try to appear otherwise than
as nature has made us."
Later books attempt the same kind of thing, but
without the bloom of freshness. In *The Patchwork Girl*
we encounter the Horners and the Hoppers, mortal
enemies because of a disagreement in taste. The former
decorate the insides of their houses and let the outsides

alone, while the latter, who are by far the odder since they have only a single leg and locomotion is by hopping, do the opposite. But Baum is not content to rest with the implications called up by the It's-what's-inside-that-counts versus It's-what-shows-that-counts argument. His further point, however, becomes blurred when the two races threaten to go to war over a pun. A Horner explains that one of his countrymen has said the Hoppers "have less understanding than we, because they've only one leg. . . . If you stand on your legs, and your legs are under you, then—ha, ha, ha!—then your legs are your under-standing. . . . And the stupid Hoppers couldn't see it."

And probably neither could the children, it seems fair to add, without the assistance of Baum's heavy hand here. And after they *have* seen it, what then?

If any doubt remains that the gimmick is running thin, consider the account in *The Lost Princess* in which the Thists are thistle-eaters with gold throats and stomachs to accommodate their diet, an eccentricity which seems to exist for its own sake.

In the same book we also see the demise of the animal-machine mentioned earlier. While the mechanical bird cannot approach the Gump, it is still a cut above the auto-dragon, "a car drawn by a gorgeous jeweled dragon, which moved its head to right and left and flashed its eyes like the headlights of an automobile and uttered a growling noise as it slowly moved toward them." One recalls the Ork, Quox, even the Wheelers with fond regret.

As much as anything else, Baum's humor also shows the strain of the long exposure. In the beginning the author's keen sense of the ridiculous provides some exceptional situation comedy, as when the Pumpkinhead confronts the Scarecrow for the first time (*Land*).

'Why, I don't understand your language. You see, I came from the Country of the Gillikins, so that I am a foreigner.'

'Ah, to be sure,' exclaimed the Scarecrow. 'I myself speak the language of the Munchkins, which is also the language of the Emerald City. But you, I suppose, speak the language of the Pumpkinheads?'

'Exactly so, your Majesty,' replied the other, bowing, 'so it will be impossible for us to understand one another.'

'That is unfortunate, certainly,' said the Scarecrow, thoughtfully. 'We must have an interpreter.'[73]

Occasionally, too, the successful Baum humor hints of Oscar Wilde[74] in its simple but blandly outrageous statements (" 'I am a king, and the promises of kings should never be relied upon,' said the old Mifket . . ."), though without Wilde's underlying gloominess. Evidently Baum's own favorite form of humor, however, is the elaborate punning which begins in earnest with *Land*, and enlivens succeeding books before sloping off after reaching a peak in *The Emerald City*.

Sir Pryse Bocks calls John Dough "a friend in knead . . . a Pan-American," and the Scarecrow says of his cornfields: "The corn I grow is always husky, and I call the ears my regiments because they have so many kernels. Of course I cannot ride my cobs. . . ."

In general Baumian humor does not date, for it is kept scrupulously non-topical. An exception are the occasional "Spoonerisms," usually confined to proper names. A modern child reader is not likely to see anything funny in a laureate versifier (*John Dough*) named Sir Austed Alfrin unless he is extremely well-read.

To replace the successful situational humor and more or less successful punning, Baum in later books fell back upon the nonsense verse which formed the substance of his first successful children's book (*Father Goose*). But in this field he is no Gilbert, or even a Gelett Burgess. A later book, *Rinkitink,* features a principal character of calculated humor, King Rinkitink of Gilgad. Falstaffian in appearance, Rinkitink simply does not live up to his comic role, for he contributes nothing but a constant laugh and a spate of unfunny comic verse (if this is not a contradiction). ("A sunny day succeeds the night;/ It's summer—then it snows!/ Right oft goes wrong and wrong comes right,/ as ev-ry wise man knows.") Falstaff-Rinkitink also owns a talking goat, who constantly tells him he is a crashing bore, if not in these exact words. But the astute child will already have perceived the truth of this, and the unfunniness of Rinkitink as expressed by the goat is not sufficient to sustain the whole book. The unfunny comic verse is also a feature of several of the other post-*Emerald City* stories. Scraps the Patchwork Girl is a jingle-maker. Even the Scarecrow falls into the habit.

One other area in which Baum shows decline probably because of the sheer length of his series lies in his handling of evil. We have seen that he is an optimistic relativist in this realm. In the introduction to *The Wizard* he expresses his intent in this matter by announcing that his story "aspires to being a modernized fairy tale, in which the wonderment and joy are retained and the heart-aches and nightmares are left out." In the main the promise is kept. But again a close look at the beginning and end of the group of Oz and Oz-related stories shows a rising tide of cruelty as well as use of the nightmare itself as episode.

The multiple deaths of the many enemies in *The Wizard*, though massive (the bees, the crows, the kalidahs), are bloodless, as is the incident in *Queen Zixi* (an early book) in which the Lord High Executioner, who has a magically extendable arm so he can reach any distance, lops off the heads of two Roly-Rogues. The latter are rather more like basketballs than creatures in any case. And when the Wizard (*Dorothy and the Wizard*) slices the body of the Mangaboo sorcerer in half to prevent his casting an evil spell, "Dorothy screamed and expected to see a terrible sight; but as the two halves of the Sorcerer fell apart on the floor she saw that he had no bones or blood inside of him at all, and that the place where he was cut looked much like a sliced turnip or potato." Aside from the fact that the earlier Dorothy would certainly not have screamed, the placing of the Mangaboos in the vegetable rather than the animal kingdom seems to save the situation, especially since they are definitely inimical to the Oz party.

This book, however, fourth of the series, seems to mark the turning of the tide. That is, enemies heretofore have not been really "bad." The girl army in *Land* is never much of a real threat, and Mombi in the same book is never allowed to carry out her wicked plans. In *Ozma* the Nomes are mild and courteous and the worst they can do seems to be transforming the animate characters into bric-a-brac, a state from which they are easily changed back. And in the same book the Wheelers, as we have seen, turn out to be nothing but noise.

Similarly, out of Oz, when the Mifket king bites off John Dough's fingers one by one, there is no real sense of mayhem, for John *is* gingerbread after all.

The entire adventure in *Dorothy and the Wizard*, on the other hand, consists of a series of encounters with enemies whose apparent intent is to destroy the protagonal party utterly. The Mangaboos leave them (the Oz group) for dead, sealed in a dark pit, the Gargoyles (which Dorothy, at home now with her new affectation, calls "Gurgles") are hideous wooden carvings with detachable wooden wings. And since it in this case evidently takes evil to match evil, contrary to normal Ozian expectation, the Wizard—surprisingly even so— appears with a brace of revolvers to counterattack. The invisible bears are carnivorous. They have already eaten the champion of the invisible people in the Valley of Voe (Woe?), who describe the incident: "When the Champion killed a bear everyone could see it; and when the bears killed the Champion we all saw several pieces of him scattered about, which of course disappeared again when the bears devoured them." The Dragon- ettes too would have devoured the party if the animals had been left unchained. It is the sheer number of absolutely vicious enemies in this book, combined with the underground, gloomy mise-en-scene, which gives an over-all effect of oppressiveness and lowering evil.

The Road to Oz, which follows, has a similar prob- lem of antagonists who are wholly evil, the Scoodlers. They take off their own heads, which have a black face on one side, a white one on the other, and use them as missiles against their enemies, whom they want to catch —or so they say—so that they (the enemies) can be boiled up for soup. During what can only be called a classic nightmare sequence in which they have thrown their two-faced heads and are trying to recover them, Toto, Dorothy's dog, steals one of the heads and runs, preventing the head from seeing its body with either of its pairs of eyes.   The other Scoodlers thereupon pelt the dog with their own heads until Toto is forced to surrender, but Dorothy's party finally triumphs by throwing all the heads down a cliff so steep they cannot be recovered by the helpless bodies.

The Nomes themselves become increasingly vicious, beginning with mere threats in *The Emerald City* (" 'Please take General Crinkle to the torture chamber. There you will kindly slice him into thin slices.   Afterward you may feed him to the seven-headed dogs.' "). By the eighth book, *Tik-Tok*, these perennial archenemies have torture implements: "great golden pincers, and prods of silver and clamps and chains and various wicked-looking instruments, all made of precious metals and set with diamonds and rubies."

And in the still later *Rinkitink* they are capable of harassing the hero, Prince Inga, with a nightmare even worse than the Scoodler incident provides.   Trapped in the vast black caverns of the Nomes, Inga feels the floor sinking beneath him in a narrow passage.   He grasps the rocky sides of a wall as a crash resounds, ending in the noise of a rushing torrent below; he lights a match to discover the floor he has just been standing on has fallen into the Bottomless Gulf.   Finally arriving at the only exit, he finds the way barred by a vast floor of white-hot coals.   The descent to the underworld is of course a classic mythic device, and to a Jungian psychologist represents the retreat into the unconscious during sleep.   The lavish descriptions of jeweled caverns of the Nomes and the opulence of their metal forest— descriptions which go beyond even those of the Emerald

City—are extremely appropriate to this concept of the place where riches are hidden from the light of consciousness, and so is the evil nature of the Nomes themselves, representatives of the unconscious deeps. So, for that matter, is the nightmare itself. The problem here is that these are certainly not tales with "the nightmares left out." On the contrary.

True, the evil in Baum never does triumph, nor does the blood ever actually flow. The degeneration here is a matter of an increase in the fright level, and a corresponding decrease in taste.

★   ★   ★   ★   ★

To summarize: probably no two Oz readers would fail to concur in a judgment that *The Wizard* is the best of all Oz books. Action is constant, the characters live, the plot is tightly managed, and the outcome immensely satisfactory. Above all, the allegory is sustained throughout.

Beside *The Wizard*, even *The Land of Oz* must take second place, although it too is a well conceived adventure, with allegorical overtones and a convincing set of characters. *Ozma of Oz* is less original; perhaps its best points are the introduction of two new characters (Tik-Tok and Billina) who come up in nearly every way to the standards of the earlier ones, and one of Baum's happier applications of the death-rebirth theme, in the descent to the underworld and return. In *Dorothy and the Wizard* this descent is abused by its very length and the near-horrors provided by purely evil enemies, while *The Road to Oz* errs in the other direction: it is little more than a casual excursion which ends in a party, to which Baum invites many of the characters from all his other fairy-tale books. While the quest pattern, now familiar, is preserved, there seems insufficient motivation for the sparse action here.

As if to make up for this very flaw, *The Emerald City* employs a double-quest plot; while the invaders of Oz are proceeding toward the city to destroy it, Dorothy and her party are junketing about Oz in an attempt to show Aunt Em and Uncle Henry the wonders. The stories are told in alternating chapters and suspense is sustained because the excursionists are happily oblivious to their danger until the last possible moment.

A more formal employment of the pattern appears in *The Patchwork Girl*. The reason for Ojo's long and trouble-fraught journey to the Emerald City is a valid one: he wants to save his uncle's life, and he exhibits the same sort of courage and resourcefulness shown by Dorothy in the first book. The Patchwork Girl herself is probably the last of Baum's truly successful inventions in the weird-character department. And these items may add up to making this the last of the really successful Oz books.

Probably because it was conceived first as a stage musical, *Tik-Tok* is little more than a reworking of the tailings of Baum's earlier and more successful "strikes." It begins with shipwreck, as does *Ozma*; the people of Oogaboo pick everything they need from trees, as do the people of Mo (and as Dorothy picks the dinner pails in *Ozma*; McKinley's slogan in the election campaign of 1900 had been "the full dinnerpail"). Ann Soforth's army has sixteen officers and one private, and is almost a match for Ozma's army with its twenty-seven officers and one private—but not quite. As in *Dorothy and the Wizard*, the protagonists pick a ruler from a plant in a vegetable kingdom. And once again there is the descent to the underworld to rescue someone imprisoned there (Offenbach's *Orpheus in Hades* was very popular at the time) as there had been in *Ozma*.

The other six books trail off into various degrees of paleness. *Rinkitink* is a fairy story which has practically nothing to do with Oz (some sources say it was an earlier story pulled into the series with minor rewriting), but this is no failing in either *John Dough* or *Queen Zixi*; both are imaginative and humorous. And this is probably the root of the problem: as we have seen, in the later books both the imagination and the humor have worn out.

★   ★   ★   ★   ★

Further, Oz-as-eden can now be seen to be Baum's greatest strength and greatest weakness. So long as the paradise remains in its prelapsarian state, the mother-goddess reigns unchallenged; it is only after the Fall that Eve becomes subject to her husband and the patriarchal Judeo-Christian cycle begins, with its consequent sorrows and responsibilities. And yet to remain in the Garden, never to emerge, is never to grow; it is recounting the myth (life to death) and leaving out half the story (death to rebirth). Any return to the womb is a regress to death, any attempt to exist in the static atmosphere of a state of perfect existence leads inevitably to tedium and nothingness. Where there can be no growth in any direction, there can be no freshness of change. Dorothy, because she could not grow up, could only deteriorate; Oz, always green, can never provide the cyclical miracle of the seasons.

> It is obvious that the infantile fantasies which we all cherish still in the unconscious play continually into myth, fairy tale, and the teachings of the church, as symbols of inde-structible being. This is helpful, for the mind feels at home with the images, and seems to be remembering something already known. But the circumstance is obstructive too, for the feelings come to rest in the symbols and resist passionately every effort to go beyond. The prodigious gulf between those childishly blissful multitudes who fill the world with piety and the truly free breaks open at the line where the symbols give way and are transcended.[75]

That the author himself realized this is not un-likely. The Lonesome Duck in the last Oz book Baum completed himself, *The Magic of Oz*, is a Baumian Tithonus, with the sentence of immortality upon him. There can be no doubt of the sincerity of the Duck's *cri de coeur*:

> 'I've lived a long time, and I've got to live forever, because I belong in the Land of Oz, where no living thing dies. Think of existing year after year, with no friends, no family, and nothing to do! Can you wonder I'm lonesome?'[76]

★   ★   ★   ★   ★

Playing the game of "if" is not always productive. And yet *if* Baum had stood by his original intention of making the *Wizard* a story without sequel, the result might have solved the problem of a bleak and changeless immortality. For Dorothy completes the cycle in that tale and returns to Kansas renewed, reborn, ready to grow up at last. On the other hand, such an early cut-off on Oz would have denied us *Ozma of Oz* and *The Emerald City*.

And *if* failing the first attempt the author had succeeded in his plan to halt the series with this latter work? Well, the damage so far as librarians and critics go had already been done by then; Oz was established as a series and hence was already by definition suspect .if not actually tainted. Such an "if" would, however, have perhaps afforded Oz a less ignominious end than it had when Baum's powers began to fail from exhaustion. Nor would any really successful Oz book have been lost unless one counts *Patchwork Girl*.

There is an "if" of another kind, too, for which close readers of Oz may entertain some regret. *If* Baum had been a little more sure of his own taste and less easily influenced by publishers, producers, other writers, his own illustrators (in particular John R. Neill whose easy, popular style was essentially inimical to the original concept of Oz), then some of the failings might at least have been staved off for a longer time. But he was essentially a crowd pleaser, as we have seen, a genial personality who selflessly tried to accommodate the whims of others whenever he could, not so much an innovator (at least in this sense) as a student of popular trends.

Perhaps in the end the real wonder of L. Frank Baum is that, of the hundreds of things he wrote, under pressure and otherwise, as many as six or seven books have proved so durable. And promise to go on enduring.

For there seems every reason to predict a future for Oz as impressive as its distinguished past. The quest for the land to the west is after all no ephemeral enthusiasm confined to the pages of history and forgotten with the closing of the frontier, but something built into occidental civilization. So long as children are born into a culture with one eye still on the vanishing Great American Desert, then those children will be unconsciously intrigued by its mysteries whether it is called Antilia or Brasil or Lovo or Capraria or Oz, or Jupiter or Planet "X" whose orbit encircles some far sun as yet uncharted by astronomers.

In a twentieth-century-plus world where Nomes and Whimsies and Growlywogs abound, there will surely always be readers wanting to know more of the wonderful wizard, the marvelous land.

NOTES, PART I

(All page references to Oz books are from Reilly & Lee editions.)

[1] New York: Coward McCann & Geoghegan, 1971. The commune is also the subject of an article by Houriet, "Life and Death of a Commune Called Oz," *New York Times Magazine*, 16 Feb 1969, pp. 31, 89-103.

[2] *The Patchwork Girl of Oz*, p. 185.

[3] pp. 1-2.

[4] *The Greening of America* (New York: Random House, 1970), p. 17. While it is not one of the primary intentions of this section to compare Baum, Populist social critic, with Reich, contemporary social critic, Reich's work is useful as a guide to overall countercultural thought, a recent comprehensive account of the current generation.

[5] Gerald Dworkin, "The Hippies: Permanent Revolution?" *Dissent* March-April 1969, p. 182.

[6] *The Land of Oz*, p. 149.

[7] *The Road to Oz*, p. 171. The passage paraphrased is, of course, ". . . for a living dog is better than a dead lion." (Ecc. 9.4.)

[8] *Road*, p. 73. Italics, RM.   [9] *Land*, p. 182.

[10] p. 148.   [11] p. 222.

[12] Reich, p. 226 (this quotation and the inset which follows).

[13] p. 130.   [14] Reich, p. 236.

[15] cf. *The Wizard of Oz*, p. 161, on the repair of the Woodman after his adventure with the winged monkeys: "To be sure there were several patches on him, but the tinsmiths did a good job, and as the Woodman was not a vain man he did not mind

174

the patches at all." And *Land*, p. 117, where the Scarecrow says of the Woodman: "My friend was ever inclined to be a dandy, and I suppose he is now more proud than ever of his personal appearance." As for the "putz-pomade" (*Land*, p. 117), in certain German-derived dialects "putz" is a vernacular term for the male sex organ, as well as a verb meaning "to brush," or "to primp." This may or may not add up to one of Baum's puns aimed over the heads of child readers, but it should be kept in mind that the author had German-speaking grandparents and other "Pennsylvania Dutch" connections.

[16] p. 56. (Until late in the series, Baum could not decide whether or not "Shaggy Man" required upper-case initials.)

[17] *Road*, p. 53.

[18] *Road*, p. 199.

[19] Reich, p. 250.

[20] *The Magic of Oz*, p. 178.

[21] *Magic*, p. 204.

[22] *Patchwork Girl*, p. 133.

[23] *Road*, pp. 23-4.

[24] *Road*, p. 210.

[25] p. 92.

[26] p. 54.

[27] pp. 164-5.

[28] "Hallelujah, I'm a Bum!" *The American Songbag*, ed. Carl Sandburg (New York: Harcourt, Brace, 1927), p. 184. A headnote by Sandburg places this song "at the water tanks of railroads in Kansas in 1897," but he adds that it was the IWW which later made it famous.

[29] Reich, p. 242.

[30] Reich, p. 224.

[31] Reich, p. 240.

[32] *Emerald City*, p. 97.

[33] p. 56.

[34] p. 60.

[35] "Ferdinando and Elvira." *Plays and Poems of W. S. Gilbert* (New York: Random House, 1932), p. 939. (Orig. pub. in *Fun*, c.1861, and later in *Bab Ballads*, 1869.)

[36] p. 119.

[37] p. 88.

[38] Reich, p. 262.

[39] *Tik-Tok of Oz*, p. 161-2.

[40] "The Flowering of the Hippies," *Atlantic*, Sept. 1967, p. 67.

[41] "Mrs. Hinck," in Miss DeFord's collection *Elsewhere, Elsewhen, Elsehow* (New York: Walker & Co., 1971).

[42] Harris, p. 71.

[43] *Tik-Tok*, p. 87.

[44] *Emerald City*, p. 268.

[45] pp. 27-8.

[46] A 1967 story by Arthur C. Clarke in *Transatlantic Review* mentions the Tin Man. A novel by James Leo Herlihy, *The Season of the Witch* (New York: Simon & Schuster, 1971), contains the expression ". . . happy in a Land of Oz." (p. 335).

Joseph S. Loventhal, Jr., in *Power and Put-on: The Law in America* (New York: Outerbridge & Dienstfrey, 1970) says: "But, like the Wizard of Oz, the [parole] officer's success [at verifying the parolee's activities] ultimately depends upon . . . parolee-faith in his, the officer's, omnipotence and on his ability to fool the parolee." Jeremy Bernstein in *The Wildest Dreams of Kew* (New York: Simon & Schuster, 1970) hints of a tremendously wide Baum audience' with: "The library [of Nepalese Field Marshal Kaiser Shamsar Rana], reputed to have been the largest private library in Asia . . . is incredibly eclectic, ranging from *The Wizard of Oz.* . . ." And Reich himself remarks: "There is a great discovery awaiting those who choose a new set of values—a discovery comparable to the revelation that the Wizard of Oz was just a humbug." (p. 348, op. cit.)

[47] *New Statesman*, 10 Sept. 1971, p. 339.

[48] Issue of 22 Oct. 1970; the cartoonist was Dunagin; rpt. in the *Baum Bugle*, Winter, 1970, p. 26.

[49] Frank Joslyn Baum and Russell P. MacFall, *To Please a Child* (Chicago: Reilly & Lee, 1961), p. 196n.

[50] "Utopia Americana," *University of Washington Chapbook* 28; republished in slightly altered form in Wagenknecht's *As Far as Yesterday* (Norman: University of Oklahoma Press, 1968).

[51] "The Wizard of Chittenango," *The New Republic*, 12 Dec. 1934, pp. 81, 141.

[52] Issue of 3 Feb. 1940; quoted by the *Baum Bugle*, Autumn, 1969.

[53] Dr. Nye is Distinguished Professor of English, Michigan State College, Lansing.

[54] East Lansing: Michigan State University Press.

[55] Cpr. 1950 by Fantasy Fiction, Inc. The story has since been anthologized several times.

[56] *American Quarterly*, Vol. 16, 1964, pp. 47-58.

[57] Chicago: Reilly & Lee.

[58] Martin Gardner in "We're Off to See the Wizard," *New York Times Book Review*, 2 May 1971, p. 1, says, ". . . 5,000,000 copies is a low estimate." Roland Baughman in "L. Frank Baum and the 'Oz Books'," *Columbia Library Columns*, May 1955, p. 27, "more than nine million copies." Dick Martin in "The Wonderful World of Oz," *Hobbies*, May 1964, 108, says "some nine million." Daniel P. Mannix in "The Father of the Wizard of Oz," *American Heritage* v. 16, p. 37, says "over

5,000,000."

[59] *The Wizard of Oz* appeared in Russia in 1939 as *The Wizard of the Emerald City,* credited not to Baum, however, but to "A. Volkov," presumably Soviet children's writer Alexander Melenlivich Volkov. Certain changes had been made; for instance, an iron woodman appears as the friend of a little girl named Ellie and her dog Totoshka. Ellie's house, a trailer with the wheels removed, is transported in a windstorm to a "Magical Country" not precisely identified as Oz. Several editions appeared, with various illustrators. The 1959 edition announced a forthcoming sequel by Volkov, *Oorfene Deuce and His Wooden Soldiers;* it appeared in Moscow in 1963, and though it features Dorothy and other Oz principals in recognizable form, the story seems to be entirely Volkov's. For some of this information I am indebted to Douglas G. and David L. Green, who included it in their introduction to the Opium Press (English language) edition (Hong Kong, 1963), translated by Mary G. Langford and titled *The Wooden Soldiers of Oz.* In this same introduction the Greenes have a quite accurate assessment of the Russian version of Oz: "Alexander Volkov's Magical Land is a kind of Looking-Glass Oz. Everything has a vague familiarity; yet, to an Oz enthusiast, nothing is quite right."

[60] MacFall, p. 280.

[61] Gardner, "The Librarians in Oz," *Saturday Review of Literature* 11 Apr. 1959, p. 18.

[62] Ibid. *supra.*

[63] "Have You Been to See the Wizard?" *Top of the News,* publication of the American Library Association, Nov. 1970, p. 41.

[64] *Bugle,* Vol. 1, No. 1, June 1957, p. 4.

[65] Reported in the *Bugle,* Nov.-Dec. 1968.

[66] Hendry Peart (pseud.), *Red Falcons of Tremoine* (New York: Knopf, 1956), and *The Loyal Grenvilles* (New York: Knopf, 1958). Miss Peart, who has also been assistant to a literary agent and has worked in bookstores in New York City and Bermuda, is now young people's librarian at Pacific Grove Public Library, Pacific Grove, California.

[67] Prentice, p. 40.

[68] Reported in the *Bugle,* Winter 1968, p. 19.

★   ★   ★   ★   ★

NOTES, PART II

[1] p. 280.

[2] With an Irish "melodrama," *The Maid of Arran*, 1882.

[3] *The Wizard*, p. 50.

[4] *Patchwork Girl*, p. 152.   [5] *Ozma*, p. 232.

[6] *Land*, p. 280.   [7] p. 175.

[8] Daniel P. Mannix, "The Father of the Wizard of Oz," *American Heritage* v. 16, Dec. 1964, p. 38.

[9] MacFall, p. 24.

[10] Michigan Military Academy, Orchard Lake, Mich.

[11] Gardner & Nye, p. 1.   [12] MacFall, p. 24.

[13] Gardner & Nye, p. 30.

[14] Here again Baum's reading was hardly extraordinary. MacFall points out that between 1888 and 1900 no less than sixty utopian novels were published.

[15] pp. 104-5.   [16] MacFall, p. 33.

[17] MacFall, p. 45.   [18] Hartford: H.H. Stoddard.

[19] The Buff Orpington has pink legs and feet, the Buff Plymouth Rock yellow. On p. 29 Billina's legs look pinkish; on p. 69 they are a definite yellow. But they turn pink again on p. 209, and yellow again on p. 216.

[20] These selections are from an early Hill edition owned by San Jose State University Library.

[21] pp. 6-7.

[22] "Autobiography of R. S. Baum, Part II," *Baum Bugle*, Spring, 1971, p. 56.

[23] *Chicago Tribune*, 26 June 1904, Sec. IV, p. 1.

[24] "Off to See the Wizard," *Bugle*, Spring, 1969, pp. 5-10.

[25] p. 154.

[26] In the letters of Maud Baum, privately printed under the title *In Other Lands than Ours*, Chicago, 1907.

[27] *The World at My Shoulder*, New York: Macmillan, 1938, p. 14.

[28] David L. Greene, "The Writing of Two L. Frank Baum Fantasies," *Bugle*, Autumn 1971, p. 14.

[29] *Chicago Tribune*, 16 Aug. 1911; quoted by Gardner & Nye, p. 38.

[30] New York: Bobbs-Merrill, 1969.

[31] *Ellery Queen's Mystery Magazine*, Nov. 1954, p. 42.

[32] *Ellery Queen*, p. 48.   [33] Gardner & Nye, p. 42 n.3

[34] *Emerald City*, pp. 21-2.   [35] Gardner & Nye, p. 29.

[36] *Emerald City*, p. 29.   [37] p. 14.

[38] p. 162.   [39] p. 238.

[40] p. 80.   [41] p. 150.

[42] *Emerald City*, pp. 258-9.   [43] p. 211.

[44] *Patchwork Girl*, p. 329.

[45] Among them Eunice Tietjens, p. 14, op. cit.

[46] Italics, RM.

[47] *New Yorker*, 19 Aug. 1939, p. 52.

★   ★   ★   ★   ★

NOTES, PART III

[1] L. Sprague DeCamp and Willy Ley, *Discoverers Before Columbus* (New York & Toronto: Rinehart & Co., 1952), p. 3.

[2] *The European Discovery of America: The Northern Voyages* (New York: Oxford University Press, 1971), p. 98.

[3] p. 91. The Ork itself may have mythic derivations. See Ruth Berman's "Here an Orc, There an Ork," *Mythlore*, Jan. 1969.

[4] Morison, p. 104.   [5] Morison, p. 103.

[6] John R. R. Tolkien, *The Lord of the Rings* (trilogy), (New York: Houghton-Mifflin, 1956-60); George Barr McCutcheon, *Graustark: The Story of a Love Behind a Throne* (first book of a series), (Chicago: Herbert S. Stone & Co., 1901); reference in sentence following: C. S. Lewis, *Chronicles of Narnia* (six books), (New York: Macmillan, 1950-56).

[7] p. 16.   [8] Gardner & Nye, p. 5.

[9] *Archetypal Patterns in Poetry* (London: Oxford University Press, 1963) p. 137. (First published 1934.)

[10] *Emerald City*, p. 30.   [11] *Patchwork Girl*, p. 20.

[12] At least we are told several times that the Emerald City is the only urban area; in *Land*, however, "the City of the Winkies" is mentioned (p. 115). It evidently disappears like Hy-Brasil immediately after this time, however, for in the next

books the Winkie country, like the rest of exurban Oz, is all pastoral. In *The Emerald City* it is made clear that "all the surrounding country, extending to the borders of the desert which enclosed it upon every side, was full of pretty and comfortable farmhouses, in which resided those inhabitants of Oz who preferred country to city life." (p. 30)

[13] *Emerald City*, p. 29.

[14] *Emerald City*, p. 30; italics, RM.

[15] p. 71.   [16] p. 178.

[17] *The Well Wrought Urn* (New York: Reynal & Hitchcock, 1947), p. 89.

[18] p. 81.   [19] pp. 32-3.

[20] p. 162.   [21] p. 120.

[22] p. 172.   [23] p. 218.

[24] p. 261.   [25] p. 235.

[26] p. 237.   [27] p. 238.

[28] p. 165.   [29] pp. 196-7.

[30] p. 198.

[31] This and following quotation, p. 200.

[32] This and foregoing quotation, p. 229.

[33] p. 232.   [34] p. 124.

[35] *Erewhon* and *Erewhon Revisited* (New York: Modern Library, 1955) pp. 88-9. (Originally published in 1872.)

[36] pp. 156-7.   [37] p. 48.

[38] *Ozma*, p. 103.   [39] p. 156.

[40] Publishing information in n. 6, Part III.

[41] *supra*, p. 90.   [42] *Graustark*, p. 104.

[43] "Off to See the Wizard," Part II, *Bugle* Spring 1969, p. 7.

[44] "The Meaning of 'Oz'," *Bugle* Autumn 1971, p. 18.

[45] In his preface to *Who's Who in Oz* (Chicago: Reilly & Lee, 1954).

[46] *The Mythmakers* (Athens: Ohio University Press, 1966), p. 144.

[47] *The Hero with a Thousand Faces* (Cleveland: World Publishing Company, Meridian Books, 1956), pp. 44-5. (Original copyright 1949 by Bollingen Foundation, New York.)

[48] Campbell, p. 132n.   [49] Campbell, pp. 113-4.

[50] p. 266.   [51] p. 60.

[52] p. 169.   [53] p. 168.

[54] pp. 152-3.   [55] *Patchwork Girl*, p. 187.

a vegetable people who live in a glass city. They are joined by the Wizard and after many perilous episodes the party arrives safely in Oz.

*The Road to Oz. Chicago: Reilly and Britton, 1909. A Kansas country crossroads is magically scrambled, causing Dorothy and her friends, the Shaggy Man, Button-Bright, and Polychrome, to travel through some curious country before reaching Oz, where Ozma is having a birthday party.

*The Emerald City of Oz. Chicago: Reilly and Britton, 1910. A double plot follows Dorothy, Aunt Em, and Uncle Henry on a tour of Oz while the Nome King and his allies plot its overthrow. The book marks the high point in Baum's development of Oz-as-utopia.

The Sea Fairies. Chicago: Reilly and Britton, 1911. An undersea adventure with Trot and Cap'n Bill, who visit the kingdom of the mermaids.

Sky Island. Chicago: Reilly and Britton, 1912. A companion piece to Fairies (above); a magic umbrella bears Trot, Cap'n Bill, and Button-Bright to a land in the sky.

*The Patchwork Girl of Oz. Chicago: Reilly and Britton, 1913. A life-sized rag doll and an animated glass cat accompany Ojo the Munchkin boy to the Emerald City to seek the salvation of Ojo's Unc Nunkie, who has been accidentally turned to stone.

*Tik-Tok of Oz. Chicago: Reilly and Britton, 1914. Betsy Bobbin is shipwrecked on the Nonestic Ocean with Hank the mule and drifts ashore in the Rose Kingdom, where people grow on bushes. They meet the Shaggy Man and go with him to the

[56] Reported in Campbell, p. 344.

[57] These and other stories of the elixir quest are available in Campbell, p. 178f.

[58] Campbell, p. 259.

[59] There was for many years a Nikobob Restaurant on Western Avenue, Los Angeles.

[60] p. 220.   [61] Patchwork Girl, p. 37.

[62] The word "robot" seems to have appeared for the first time in literature in Capek's RUR.

[63] "The Father of the Wizard of Oz," American Heritage Dec. 1964, p. 108.

[64] Gardner & Nye, p. 3.   [65] Wizard, p. 213.

[66] Ozma, p. 94.

[67] Among writers remarking about this has been Dick Martin, "The Wonderful World of Oz," Hobbies May 1959, p. 1-7. The full sentence reads: "Although his Wizard and his other books are not masterpieces of literary style, he possessed a flawless command of English, and his narratives are written with a dignity, grace and ease not often found in children's books." Strangely (because the statement has so little supporting evidence) the assertion is repeated almost verbatim (though not directly credited) by Ann E. Prentice (op. cit., p. 36): "He used words with a flawless command of English and his stories are written with a dignity, grace, and ease not usually found in children's books."

[68] Wizard, pp. 154-5.   [69] p. 270.

[70] pp. 255-6.   [71] p. 241.

[72] pp. 233-4.   [73] p. 68.

[74] Especially the Wilde of The Happy Prince and Other Stories (London: Duckworth, 1935). (Originally published 1888.)

[75] Campbell, p. 177.   [76] p. 178.

PRIMARY BIBLIOGRAPHY

(The Oz series books are marked with an asterisk.)

*The Wonderful Wizard of Oz. Chicago: George M. Hill, 1900. Dorothy, an ingenious little girl; the Cowardly Lion, a brave beast; the Tin Woodman, a compassionate tin man, and the Scarecrow, who is very wise, apply to the Wizard of Oz for the qualities they imagine they lack. Republished subsequently as The Wizard of Oz.

The Enchanted Island of Yew. Indianapolis: Bobbs-Merrill, 1903. Marvel, a fairy prince, sets out on an adventure through the kingdoms of Yew. He vanquishes King Terribus by kindness and, among other things, meets the High Ki of Twi and saves his friends from the Red Rogue before returning to the fairy realm from which he (she) came.

*The Marvelous Land of Oz. Chicago: Reilly and Britton, 1904. Tip, a small boy, runs away from the witch Mombi, taking Jack Pumpkinhead and the Saw Horse; they go to consult the Scarecrow, wisest man in Oz and its then ruler, about their problems, but arrive at the Emerald City in time to help save it from invasion by General Jinjur and her all-girl army.

Queen Zixi of Ix. New York: Century, 1905. A magic cloak, provided at the whim of fairies, grants one wish to each wearer and causes Queen Zixi, six hundred and eighty-three years old but able by enchantment to pass for eighteen, to go to war with King Bud of Noland. Invasion of Noland by the Roly-Rogues subsequently forces Zixi to come to Bud's aid. Zixi never does get her wish from the cloak—she wanted to be able to look without horror into a mirror; mirrors don't lie and her reflection showed her true age—but she does learn something valuable: not to try to change the unchangeable.

John Dough and the Cherub. Chicago: Reilly and Britton, 1906. A whimsical French-American baker creates a human-sized gingerbread man to celebrate the Fourth of July; he is brought to life by The Great Elixir, and accidentally but appropriately dispatched to the Isle of Phreex by a holiday rocket. There this hero is joined in his flight to escape the pursuing owner of the Elixir, Ali-Dubh, by Chick, the original incubator baby.

*Ozma of Oz. Chicago: Reilly and Britton, 1907. Dorothy arrives in the Land of Ev after being washed overboard from a steamer as she accompanies her Uncle Henry to Australia. She meets Ozma and company there and attends her to the realm of the Nomes to free the captive royal family of Ev.

*Dorothy and the Wizard in Oz. Chicago: Reilly and Britton, 1908. Dorothy and her cousin Zeb fall through a crack opened by a California earthquake and find themselves among the Mangaboos,

[56] Reported in Campbell, p. 344.

[57] These and other stories of the elixir quest are available in Campbell, p. 178f.

[58] Campbell, p. 259.

[59] There was for many years a Nikobob Restaurant on Western Avenue, Los Angeles.

[60] p. 220.   [61] *Patchwork Girl*, p. 37.

[62] The word "robot" seems to have appeared for the first time in literature in Capek's *RUR*.

[63] "The Father of the Wizard of Oz," *American Heritage* Dec. 1964, p. 108.

[64] Gardner & Nye, p. 3.   [65] *Wizard*, p. 213.

[66] *Ozma*, p. 94.

[67] Among writers remarking about this has been Dick Martin, "The Wonderful World of Oz," *Hobbies* May 1959, p. 1-7. The full sentence reads: "Although his *Wizard* and his other books are not masterpieces of literary style, he possessed a flawless command of English, and his narratives are written with a dignity, grace and ease not often found in children's books." Strangely (because the statement has so little supporting evidence) the assertion is repeated almost verbatim (though not directly credited) by Ann E. Prentice (op. cit., p. 36): "He used words with a flawless command of English and his stories are written with a dignity, grace, and ease not usually found in children's books."

[68] *Wizard*, pp. 154-5.   [69] p. 270.
[70] pp. 255-6.   [71] p. 241.
[72] pp. 233-4.   [73] p. 68.

[74] Especially the Wilde of *The Happy Prince and Other Stories* (London: Duckworth, 1935). (Originally published 1888.)

[75] Campbell, p. 177.   [76] p. 178.

PRIMARY BIBLIOGRAPHY

(The Oz series books are marked with an asterisk.)

The Wonderful Wizard of Oz. Chicago: George M. Hill, 1900. Dorothy, an ingenious little girl; the Cowardly Lion, a brave beast; the Tin Woodman, a compassionate tin man, and the Scarecrow, who is very wise, apply to the Wizard of Oz for the qualities they imagine they lack. Republished subsequently as *The Wizard of Oz.*

The Enchanted Island of Yew. Indianapolis: Bobbs-Merrill, 1903. Marvel, a fairy prince, sets out on an adventure through the kingdoms of Yew. He vanquishes King Terribus by kindness and, among other things, meets the High Ki of Twi and saves his friends from the Red Rogue before returning to the fairy realm from which he (she) came.

The Marvelous Land of Oz. Chicago: Reilly and Britton, 1904. Tip, a small boy, runs away from the witch Mombi, taking Jack Pumpkinhead and the Saw Horse; they go to consult the Scarecrow, wisest man in Oz and its then ruler, about their problems, but arrive at the Emerald City in time to help save it from invasion by General Jinjur and her all-girl army.

182

Queen Zixi of Ix. New York: Century, 1905. A magic cloak, provided at the whim of fairies, grants one wish to each wearer and causes Queen Zixi, six hundred and eighty-three years old but able by enchantment to pass for eighteen, to go to war with King Bud of Noland. Invasion of Noland by the Roly-Rogues subsequently forces Zixi to come to Bud's aid. Zixi never does get her wish from the cloak—she wanted to be able to look without horror into a mirror; mirrors don't lie and her reflection showed her true age—but she does learn something valuable: not to try to change the unchangeable.

John Dough and the Cherub. Chicago: Reilly and Britton, 1906. A whimsical French-American baker creates a human-sized gingerbread man to celebrate the Fourth of July; he is brought to life by The Great Elixir, and accidentally but appropriately dispatched to the Isle of Phreex by a holiday rocket. There this hero is joined in his flight to escape the pursuing owner of the Elixir, Ali-Dubh, by Chick, the original incubator baby.

Ozma of Oz. Chicago: Reilly and Britton, 1907. Dorothy arrives in the Land of Ev after being washed overboard from a steamer as she accompanies her Uncle Henry to Australia. She meets Ozma and company there and attends her to the realm of the Nomes to free the captive royal family of Ev.

Dorothy and the Wizard in Oz. Chicago: Reilly and Britton, 1908. Dorothy and her cousin Zeb fall through a crack opened by a California earthquake and find themselves among the Mangaboos, a vegetable people who live in a glass city. They are joined by the Wizard and after many perilous episodes the party arrives safely in Oz.

*The Road to Oz. Chicago: Reilly and Britton, 1909. A Kansas country crossroads is magically scrambled, causing Dorothy and her friends, the Shaggy Man, Button-Bright, and Polychrome, to travel through some curious country before reaching Oz, where Ozma is having a birthday party.

*The Emerald City of Oz. Chicago: Reilly and Britton, 1910. A double plot follows Dorothy, Aunt Em, and Uncle Henry on a tour of Oz while the Nome King and his allies plot its overthrow. The book marks the high point in Baum's development of Oz-as-utopia.

The Sea Fairies. Chicago: Reilly and Britton, 1911. An undersea adventure with Trot and Cap'n Bill, who visit the kingdom of the mermaids.

Sky Island. Chicago: Reilly and Britton, 1912. A companion piece to Fairies (above); a magic umbrella bears Trot, Cap'n Bill, and Button-Bright to a land in the sky.

*The Patchwork Girl of Oz. Chicago: Reilly and Britton, 1913. A life-sized rag doll and an animated glass cat accompany Ojo the Munchkin boy to the Emerald City to seek the salvation of Ojo's Unc Nunkie, who has been accidentally turned to stone.

*Tik-Tok of Oz. Chicago: Reilly and Britton, 1914. Betsy Bobbin is shipwrecked on the Nonestic Ocean with Hank the mule and drifts ashore in the Rose Kingdom, where people grow on bushes. They meet the Shaggy Man and go with him to the

Nome Kingdom to save his brother, a prisoner
there. This is also a double plot, the other half of
which follows Ann Soforth and her army in their
attempt to conquer the world. When the two
parties join forces, they are defeated (nearly) by
the Nomes, who drop them through The Tube to
the other side of the world, but the adventurers
are returned to safety by Quox, a friendly dragon,
in time to outwit the Nomes at last.

The Scarecrow of Oz. Chicago: Reilly and Britton,
1915. Trot and Cap'n Bill, in their rowboat, are
sucked by a whirlpool into a sea cavern. After
many vicissitudes they are rescued in Jinxland by
the Scarecrow and brought to the Emerald City.
Much depends on magic transformations of people
into animals and insects, and on the help of the
Ork and his friends. (According to Jack Snow's
Who's Who in Oz, Baum considered this book his
best.)

Rinkitink in Oz. Chicago: Reilly and Britton, 1916.
Accompanied by King Rinkitink and his bad-
tempered goat Bilbil (who later turns out to be a
prince under enchantment), Prince Inga of Pingaree,
one of the islands in the Nonestic Ocean, sets out
to rescue his parents, captives first of enemies from
the neighboring islands of Regos and Coregos, then
of the infamous Nomes.

The Lost Princess of Oz. Chicago: Reilly and Britton,
1917. Ozma is kidnapped by Ugu the Shoemaker,
an amateur magician, and all her magic stolen,
leaving her helpless. She is found and rescued by
Dorothy and the Wizard after her transformation
into a peach pit. The Frog Man, Cayke the Cookie-

Cook, and others are introduced in a double plot.

The Tin Woodman of Oz. Chicago: Reilly and Britton, 1918. The Woodman and Captain Fyter find their former mutual sweetheart, Nimmie Aimee, wed to Chopfyt, a flesh-and-blood man made of their chopped-off extremities.

The Magic of Oz. Chicago: Reilly and Lee, 1919. Ruggedo, the deposed Nome King, tries again to invade Oz with the help of Kiki Aru, a Munchkin boy illegally practicing magic. This is the book with the famous magic word "pyrzqxgl," which if pronounced correctly will cause magic transformations.

Glinda of Oz. Chicago: Reilly and Lee, 1920. Dorothy and Ozma become imprisoned in a crystal dome on an island submerged in a lake. Glinda comes to the rescue. There is a tense search for the magic word which will activate the machinery which raises the island. Although the publisher referred to this as "the last book written by Baum," there is reason to believe much of the final writing was done by Ruth Plumly Thompson, the first of a succession of writers employed to continue the series after Baum's death.

Note: All Oz books except *The Wizard* were illustrated by John R. Neill. *The Wizard* was illustrated by W. W. Denslow.

SECONDARY BIBLIOGRAPHY

The Book of the Hamburgs: a brief treatise upon the mating, rearing and management of the different varieties of Hamburgs. Hartford: H. H. Stoddard, 1886.

Mother Goose in Prose. Illus. Maxfield Parrish. Chicago: Way & Williams, 1897.

By the Candelabra's Glare. Illus. W. W. Denslow, et al. Chicago: pvt. pntng. by L. Frank Baum, 99 copies, 1898.

Father Goose, His Book. Illus. Denslow. Chicago: George M. Hill, 1899.

The Art of Decorating Dry Goods Windows and Interiors. Chicago: The Show Window Publishing Co., 1900.

The Army Alphabet. Illus. Harry Kennedy. Chicago: George H. Hill, 1900.

The Navy Alphabet. Illus. Kennedy. Chicago: George M. Hill, 1900.

A New Wonderland. Illus. Frank Berbeck. New York: R. H. Russell, 1900. (Later re-issued as *The Magical Monarch of Mo.*)

The Songs of Father Goose. Illus. Denslow. Music Alberta N. Hall. Chicago: George M. Hill, 1900.

American Fairy Tales. Illus. Ike Morgan, et al. Chicago: George M. Hill, 1901.

Dot and Tot of Merryland. Illus. Denslow. Chicago: George M. Hill, 1901.

The Master Key. Illus. F. Y. Cory. Indianapolis: Bowen-Merrill, 1901.

The Life and Adventures of Santa Claus. Illus. Mary Cowles Clark. Indianapolis: Bowen-Merrill, 1902.

The Surprising Adventures of the Magical Monarch of Mo. Illus. Verbeck. Indianapolis: Bobbs-Merrill, 1903. See listing on *A New Wonderland.*

The Woggle-Bug Book. Illus. Morgan. Chicago: Reilly and Britton, 1905.

Father Goose's Year Book: Quaint Quacks and Feathered Shafts for Mature Children. Illus. Walter J. Enright. Chicago: Reilly and Britton, 1907.

Baum's American Fairy Tales. Illus. George Kerr. Indianapolis: Bobbs-Merrill, 1908. Edited and expanded version of *American Fairy Tales* (see listing).

L. Frank Baum's Juvenile Speaker. Illus. John R. Neill, et al. Chicago: Reilly and Britton, 1910.

The Daring Twins. Illus. Pauline Batchelder. Chicago: Reilly and Britton, 1911.

Baum's Own Book for Children. Chicago: Reilly and Britton, 1912. Reissue of *Juvenile Speaker* (see listing).

Phoebe Daring. Illus. Joseph Pierre Nuyttens. Chicago:

Reilly and Britton, 1912.

The Little Wizard Series. (Six-volume duodecimo set for young children.) Chicago: Reilly and Britton, 1913. Reissued in 1914 in one volume, *Little Wizard Stories of Oz.*

The Snuggle Tales. (Six volumes, separately issued.) *Little Bun Rabbit*, 1916; *Once Upon a Time*, 1916; *The Yellow Hen*, 1916; *The Magic Cloak*, 1916; *The Gingerbread Man*, 1917; *Jack Pumpkinhead*, 1917. Chicago: Reilly and Britton. (The first four books are a reissue of material from the *Juvenile Speaker.* Series reprinted 1920 as *Oz-Man Tales.*

Our Landlady. Mitchell: South Dakota Writers' Project, 1941. (Selection of columns from the *Aberdeen Saturday Pioneer*, 1890-91.)

Jaglon and the Tiger Fairies. Illus. Dale Ulrey. Chicago: Reilly & Lee, 1953. (Reprint of a short story from a series in the *Delineator*, 1905.)

A Kidnapped Santa Claus. New York: Bobbs-Merrill, 1961. (Reprinted from a short story in the *Delineator*, Dec. 1904.)

Anonymous and Pseudonymous Books

The Last Egyptian. Anon. Illus. Francis P. Wightman. Philadelphia: Edward Stern, 1908.

By Floyd Akers:

The Boy Fortune Hunters in Alaska. Chicago: Reilly and Britton, 1908.

The Boy Fortune Hunters in Panama. Chicago: Reilly and Britton, 1908. (This and the book above are reissues of the Sam Steele books by "Capt. Hugh Fitzgerald." See listings *infra.*)

The Boy Fortune Hunters in Egypt. Chicago: Reilly and Britton, 1908.

The Boy Fortune Hunters in China. Chicago: Reilly and Britton, 1909.

The Boy Fortune Hunters in Yucatan. Chicago: Reilly and Britton, 1910.

The Boy Fortune Hunters in the South Seas. Chicago: Reilly and Britton, 1911.

By Laura Bancroft:

Twinkle Tales. Chicago: Reilly and Britton, 1906. (Six duodecimos for young children; reissued in 1911 as *Twinkle and Chubbins*, single volume.)

Policeman Bluejay. Chicago: Reilly & Britton, 1907. (Reissued as *Babes in Birdland*, 1911; a second reissue of this title in 1917 was under Baum's own name.)

By John Estes Cooke:

Tamawaca Folks. Pvt. Pntng. 1907.

By Capt. Hugh Fitzgerald:

Sam Steele's Adventures on Land and Sea. Chicago: Reilly and Britton, 1906. (On this and following title, see listings *supra* under Floyd Akers.)

Sam Steele's Adventures in Panama. Chicago: Reilly and Britton, 1907.

By Suzanne Metcalf:

Annabel. Chicago: Reilly and Britton, 1906.

By Schuyler Staunton:

The Fate of a Crown. Chicago: Reilly and Britton, 1905.

Daughters of Destiny. Chicago: Reilly and Britton, 1906.

By Edith Van Dyne:

Aunt Jane's Nieces. Chicago: Reilly and Britton, 1906.

Aunt Jane's Nieces Abroad. Chicago: Reilly and Britton, 1906.

Aunt Jane's Nieces at Millville. Chicago: Reilly and Britton, 1908.

Aunt Jane's Nieces at Work. Chicago: Reilly and Britton, 1909.

Aunt Jane's Nieces in Society. Chicago: Reilly and Britton, 1910.

Aunt Jane's Nieces and Uncle John. Chicago: Reilly and Britton, 1911.

The Flying Girl. Chicago: Reilly and Britton, 1911.

Aunt Jane's Nieces on Vacation. Chicago: Reilly and Britton, 1912.

The Flying Girl and her Chum. Chicago: Reilly and Britton, 1912.

Aunt Jane's Nieces on the Ranch. Chicago: Reilly and Britton, 1913.

Aunt Jane's Nieces Out West. Chicago: Reilly and Britton, 1914.

Aunt Jane's Nieces in the Red Cross. Chicago: Reilly and Britton, 1915.

Mary Louise. Chicago: Reilly and Britton, 1916.

Mary Louise in the Country. Chicago: Reilly and Britton, 1916.

Mary Louise Solves a Mystery. Chicago: Reilly and Britton, 1917.

Mary Louise and the Liberty Girls. Chicago: Reilly and Britton, 1918.

Mary Louise Adopts a Soldier. Chicago: Reilly and Britton, 1919.

Magazine and Newspaper Stories
which have not Appeared as Books

"The Suicide of Kiaros." *The White Elephant.* Sept. 1897. Rptd. *Ellery Queen's Mystery Magazine.* Nov. 1954.

"The Mating Day." *Short Stories.* Sept. 1898.

"Aunt Hulda's Good Time." *The Youth's Companion.* 26 Oct. 1899.

"The Loveridge Burglary." *Short Stories.* Jan. 1900.

"The Bad Man." *The Home Magazine.* 10 Sept. 1901.

"Queer Visitors from the Marvelous Land of Oz." 27-story series for *The Chicago Sunday Record-Herald* and other newspapers. Aug. 28, 1904-Feb. 26, 1905.

"Animal Fairy Tales." Series of nine stories. *Delineator* Jan.-Sept. 1905. (The first story appeared in *Jaglon*; see listing *supra.*)

"Nelebel's Fairyland." *The Russ.* June 1905.

"Jack Burgitt's Honor." *Novelettes.* No. 68 Aug. 1905.

"The Man Fairy." *The Ladies' World.* Dec. 1910.

"The Tramp and the Baby." *The Ladies' World.* Oct. 1911.

"Bessie's Fairy Tale." *The Ladies' World.* Dec. 1911.

"Aunt Phroney's Boy." *St. Nicholas.* Dec. 1912. (Rewritten version of "Aunt Huldah's Good Time," listing *supra.*)

"The Yellow Ryl." *A Child's Garden.* n.d.

SELECTED CRITICAL
AND BIOGRAPHICAL SOURCES

Baughman, Roland. "L. Frank Baum and the 'Oz Books'." *Columbia University Library Columns.* May 1955, pp. 14-35.

The Baum Bugle. Issues from Summer 1957 to present. Published by The International Wizard of Oz Club, Inc., Box 95, Kinderhook, Ill.

Baum, Frank L. "Why the Wizard Keeps on Selling." *Writer's Digest.* Dec. 1952.

Baum, Frank Joslyn, and MacFall, Russell P. *To Please a Child.* Chicago: Reilly and Lee Co., 1962.

Brotman, Jordan. "A Late Wanderer in Oz." *Only Connect.* Eds. Sheila Egoff, et al. New York: Oxford University Press, 1969. pp. 156-169.

Dictionary of American Biography. Auth. Muriel Shaver. New York: Scribner's, 1929. Vol. 2, p. 59.

Erisman, Fred. "L. Frank Baum and the Progressive Dilemma." *American Quarterly.* Fall, 1968, pp. 616-23.

Gardner, Martin, and Nye, Russel B. *The Wizard of Oz and Who He Was.* East Lansing: Michigan State University Press, 1957.

Gardner, Martin. "The Librarians in Oz." *Saturday Review* 42. 11 Apr. 1959, pp. 18-19.

————. "Why Librarians Dislike Oz." *Library Journal* 88. 15 Feb. 1963, pp. 834-6.

————. "A Child's Garden of Bewilderment." *Saturday Review* 48. 17 Jul. 1965, pp. 18-19.

————. "We're Off to See the Wizard." *New York Times Book Review.* 2 May 1971, pp. 1 & 42.

Littlefield, Henry M. "The Wizard of Oz: Parable on Populism." *American Quarterly* XVI. Spring 1964, pp. 47-58.

Mannix, Daniel P. "The Father of the Wizard of Oz." *American Heritage* 16. Dec. 1964, pp. 36-47.

Mayes, H. R. Trade Winds (col.). *Saturday Review* 50. 29 Jul. 1967, pp. 10-11.

Prentice, Ann E. "Have You Been to See the Wizard?" *The Top of the News* (American Library Association). 1 Nov. 1970, pp. 32-44.

Sackett, S. J. "The Utopia of Oz." *The Georgia Review.* Fall 1960.

Snow, Jack. *Who's Who in Oz.* Chicago: Reilly and Lee, 1954.

Starrett, Vincent. "The Wizard of Oz." *Best Loved Books of the Twentieth Century.* New York: Bantam, 1955.

Thurber, James. "The Wizard of Chittenango." *The New Republic.* 12 Dec. 1934, pp. 81 & 141.

Wagenknecht, Edward. "Utopia Americana." *University of Washington Chapbook* 28 (1929). Rptd. as "The Yellow Brick Road," a chapter in *As Far as Yesterday.* Norman: University of Oklahoma Press, 1968.

Who Was Who in America. Chicago: A. N. Marcus Co., 1950. Vol. I, p. 70.

INDEX

195